THE WRITINGS OF
Camilla Eyring Kimball

THE WRITINGS OF
Camilla Eyring Kimball

EDITED BY
EDWARD L. KIMBALL

Deseret Book Company
Salt Lake City, Utah

First printing March 1988

Library of Congress Catalog Card Number 88-70095
ISBN 0-87579-143-3

Contents

v

Excerpts from Camilla's Writings

Foreword

by Carolyn J. Rasmus, Administrative Assistant
to the Young Women General Presidency

Like so many other women, I tried never to miss an opportunity to hear Camilla Kimball speak and to read what she had written or what others had written about her. Her calm demeanor and the sparkle in her eyes told me she had made peace with herself and with life.

Although she preferred the quiet life, she was thrust before the public as she became "first lady of the Church" during the administration of President Kimball. Her words and example came at a time in history when women were seeking to better understand themselves and their role. She spoke often and forcefully about the significance of home and family and the responsibilities of marriage, while placing equal emphasis on the pursuit of knowledge and the importance of education. Her messages were powerful because her life evidenced the things about which she spoke. She had experienced hardship, problems, disappointment, and frustration. But she also knew of joy and discovery and love.

Ironically, this woman who sought privacy and shunned the public eye openly shared her personal struggles and used her own life experiences to illustrate her teaching. She admitted she didn't know all the answers, while repeatedly acknowledging God's role in all things. She could speak about being a faithful woman because she was one. Her very words illustrated her commitment to learning as a pleasure and a discipline of the mind.

Like her life, her spoken messages lifted and encouraged and inspired others. Camilla Eyring Kimball's writings have been compiled in this book so that others might know of this faithful woman and learn from her.

Introduction

by Edward L. Kimball

No one would be more surprised at the appearance of a book containing her words than Camilla Kimball. She said nothing that others have not said, and said perhaps as well, but because of the happy combination of her personality and her position, the words she wrote and spoke carry a little extra weight. She spent twelve years at the side of her husband, Spencer, as he filled the role of president of The Church of Jesus Christ of Latter-day Saints, years during which the Church nearly doubled in size, so that, just as for millions of Latter-day Saints Spencer W. Kimball was "the prophet," so Camilla Eyring Kimball was "the first lady" of the Church.

Her time in the spotlight coincided with a great change in society concerning the role of women. In some important way she bridged the gap. She believed in and exemplified the commitment to women's supporting role, with home and family as first responsibility. But she also believed in and exemplified that for a woman to choose or accept that role was not the same as admitting to inferior status.

She was intelligent, and while she did not parade it, neither did she deny or hide it. She was independent of spirit and stood with her husband by choice, not compulsion. She was shy, yet she learned to present herself as confident and gracious. She was refreshingly candid, not afraid to talk of her mistakes and foibles, while demonstrating by her life that those follies have little to do with ultimate success. She had a loving heart, open to those close by and those out there in the crowd. She worked hard, sweating in her garden for the satisfaction of coaxing from the soil beautiful flowers and the produce of a vegetable garden. She had a testimony of the gospel of Christ not dependent on her husband's. She had a different approach than he and had to find her own answers, in her own way. Though personally conventional and conservative, she had an unusual tolerance for difference. Easy-going in general, she could show steel-hard determination when persuaded that right required it.

A fine homemaker by training and inclination, she enjoyed needlework, cooking, sewing, and managing a household. It is not that she enjoyed all work in itself, but that she took satisfaction in fulfilling well the assignment she had accepted.

Camilla said once, "I love this life. I love the hot sun on my back as I work in the garden; I love to gather my family about me; I love parties; I love to read and explore ideas and see new places; I love to visit the Saints and sense their vibrant faith. Living in this world has proven to be a voyage of continual discovery. I am reluctant to have it end. I am having too good a time."

It did end, of course, as it must for us all. She passed away September 20, 1987, at nearly ninety-three years of age.

Until a month before her death, when she became bedfast, Camilla was abroad nearly every day, to church, to the temple, to visit friends, to a luncheon. She was in pain from arthritis much of the time, but she refused to let it stop her. She went even if it meant going in a wheelchair carrying a portable canister of oxygen. She felt that temple work was one thing she could still do for others. She served as a visiting teacher to the end, though sometimes the women to be taught had to come to her. She took up painting less than a year before she died and completed a dozen paintings of respectable quality. She could not just sit; she moved to the challenge. She read with a purpose, not for entertainment. Endlessly curious, she watched nature shows on television because it thrilled her to see the interrelationships among God's creatures. She exclaimed at the marvelous Creation, at how intricate the design, how thoughtful the Designer. She had a capacity for wonder.

Camilla's husband knew how deeply indebted he was to her for her unswerving loyalty, her support and encouragement. He said to a group of missionaries in 1959, "You go home and find a person [to marry] that will stimulate you, one that will keep you on your toes, that will make you be bigger than you are, never anyone that will let you relax. I would never be in the Council of the Twelve today if I had married some of the girls that I have know. Sister Kimball kept me growing and never let me be satisfied with mediocrity."

With all these good things said, she herself would be squirming. She knew that in many ways she was an ordinary person, capable of mistakes and author of many. She was, however, more conscious of them than the rest of us. We saw her better as a whole, while she was so close that she saw especially the flaws. In a position of prominence that she had not sought, but accepted gracefully, she remained reassuringly down to earth.

A sense of her character can best be derived from her own statements. During an interview concerning the book *Camilla*, she said, "In thinking about the publication of my life story, I have been torn between regret at the loss of privacy and gratification at people's generous response. At one point in the preparation of the book I said, 'I just don't want it. I don't want to be the object of curiosity. I need what privacy I can preserve.' But my son persuaded me that some good might come out of the publication. He urged that there were many women who looked to me as a role model and that they needed to know that a woman can be loving and supportive and still have a mind and faith of her own, without being just an appendage of a man, and that the marriage relationship between a good man and a good woman is not that of master and servant, but of two equals who share responsibility for the success of the family, simply having different assignments. I was persuaded enough to let the project go ahead. The book makes me out more of a heroine than I am. I have just tried to do my duty and enjoy life in the process. Of course, I would not be candid if I did not admit that there is some satisfaction in thinking that your life has enough interest that others want to know about it."

Another time, "I have overcome shyness with time and experience, but I still become a little concerned if we are to meet someone outside the Church who is prominent. I fear they might judge the Church by me, and I find that disconcerting. I am conscious of wanting to appear intelligent and respectable and adequately dressed, to represent the Church well."

She was an exceptional listener. She played a major role in the lives of her sons as they sat in the kitchen discussing their latest ideas, even heretical ones. She listened to it all and expressed her views. They were likely to feel they had won the debate, only to find that in later conversations with others they were echoing her ideas.

None of the children doubted their parents' unreserved love, despite times of disappointment over the children's conduct. That same unwavering love existed between them. While they sometimes disagreed, there were no harsh words.

The warm reception received by her biography, published in 1980, frankly amazed her. Though mostly it tells of the events in her life, one can get glimpses of personality, especially in statements she made without thought of public consumption.

In a letter to her husband while she was with her youngest son in California, for treatment for polio, November 14, 1933, she wrote:

My beloved husband,

The day you receive this note will mark the sixteenth anniversary of our wedding. Our first separation on that day. I wanted to tell you again as I perhaps do too often how much I love and appreciate you. Every year increases my love and respect. This separation is bitterly hard but it has made me realize more than ever before how much I have to be thankful for. The fact that never once in the time of our acquaintance have I found cause to doubt or mistrust is I consider one of the foundation stones upon which real happiness and contentment in marriage are built. The attraction of sex and other things, of course, combine to make the perfect union, but without confidence there can be nothing lasting.

I feel that our trouble has drawn us even closer together in spirit though temporarily we are separated.

My constant prayer is that God will preserve the unity of our family and that we may soon all be together again. The joy of that day will be unmeasurable.

How I long for you and the strength received from your beautiful character. There is no other so fine and so true.

Your devoted wife, Camilla

In 1936, after Spencer had been elected district governor of the Rotary Clubs of Arizona, she wrote in her journal, "It was a very pleasant experience, but I really do not crave publicity. I am satisfied to go quietly my own way. I do feel that much worthwhile development has come from the contacts through Rotary this year and I have appreciated it as an opportunity to grow. I have a real ambition to learn to be quietly at ease under any circumstances and in any company, to take my place in a dignified yet simple manner. I dislike the pompous air and I do seek to be genuinely cordial." And, in delightful irony, she added, "I never expect to come as near the center of the stage again."

After Spencer had been an apostle for several years and was traveling in Canada, Camilla expressed her feelings in a letter: "Sometimes I almost feel in the press of your many responsibilities that I don't matter very much anymore. Anyone who thinks being the wife of one of the general authorities is a bed of roses should try it once, shouldn't they? Theoretically I realize and appreciate all the blessings and advantages, but sometimes I selfishly feel it would be nice not to have to share my husband with a million others. I do love and appreciate you, dear, and admire your sterling qualities. I wouldn't have you be one whit less valiant in the pursuit of your duty, . . . but it is comforting to be reassured once in a while that you realize I am standing by."

With Spencer diagnosed in 1971 as having not only a failing heart but also recurrence of throat cancer, Camilla received comfort from a blessing under the hands of President Harold B. Lee. She wrote in her journal, "It gave me more feeling of strength and peace than I had had for a long time. I realized that I had given up hope and was allowing myself to be morbid and defeated. I tried doubly hard to be cheerful and hopeful, though I continued to have my dark moments when the tears and anguish found vent."

In 1972 she drove herself to the hospital with a perforated appendix so as not to disturb her husband at work until she had to. She wrote, "The most traumatic aspect was that I was to give the Relief Society spiritual living lesson on November 1, the day I was admitted to the hospital. There was nothing I could do but just drop it in the lap of Sister Conover, the Relief Society president. She called Sister Haglund, who gives the lesson in the First Ward, and she carried on. Everyone has said how very well she did. I didn't get one bit of consolation that I was missed at all. It is good for one to be reminded that she is not indispensable. This whole experience has taken good care of that. The world has gone smoothly on its way with no concern that I haven't been on the job."

She had the capacity for spiritual experience. After the operation came infection and a slow recovery. "When I was so discouraged, Spencer asked President Marion G. Romney if he would come in the evening and give me a special blessing. He did, and as he prayed, one statement impressed me indelibly: 'I bless you with the gift to be healed.' It was as if those words were imprinted on a banner before me. As I continued to contemplate this blessing, it was borne in upon me with greater and greater clarity that I had had a special blessing given at a time of greatest need and that it was up to me to claim that blessing. It was up to me to take courage, to determine to do everything in my power that I might have the gift to be healed. I bear my testimony to this spiritual experience and feel a great responsibility to claim this blessing."

After Spencer became president of the Church, he was felt to need round-the-clock security. Camilla wrote: "This is beginning to get on my nerves. I woke up at two A.M. when two security men were changing shifts. We had left the bedroom door partly ajar, and I could see the two of them visiting in the living room. This was almost more than I could take. I wanted to call out and tell them to please go home and leave us alone. Who would have thought that we who love our independence and our privacy so much would be surrounded by guards?"

She was capable of some pettiness: "You know, in all my life I really disliked only one person. It was a woman I could hardly stand to speak to. She was so sickly sweet, yet so self-centered. She had nothing to talk about except her husband and her children's great accomplishments. She had no life of her own and had such vanity in the reflected glory. I find I cannot recall her without distaste. May the Lord forgive me."

After a second brain operation on her husband in 1979, she confided in her journal: "It takes more than a little will power for me to keep cheerful when Spencer is melancholy. The arthritis in my knees gets increasingly worse and my shoulder is more painful all the time. At home I am nurse, housekeeper, cook, and hostess, which I am not always equal to. Sometimes I wonder how long I can keep up. I try hard not to let Spencer know how miserable I sometimes feel."

But the next year she responded to an interviewer who commiserated about all the things she had been through, "Of course there are moments of discouragement, but if you have the impression that trouble is the main theme in my life, you are mistaken. I have had a wonderful life. I have been blessed with righteous parents, a loving husband and family, generous neighbors, and stimulating friends. Spencer and I have received respect and honor. I have had challenging responsibilities and a sense of being useful to the Lord's work in at least a small way. Others suffer their share of trials too; their troubles are just different from mine. I learned long ago that with God's help there is no difficulty too great to overcome. That knowledge keeps me from being discouraged for long. Life is eternal, and our present experiences simply serve as preparation for what is to come. We cannot afford to sink into self-pity. We have too much to learn and do."

Camilla Kimball gave innumerable talks, revolving around a relatively few themes and calling repeatedly on her own experiences as a child in Mexico and as a refugee from a Mexican revolution in 1912. Her role as wife of the president of the Church called for her not to undertake doctrinal exposition so much as to help by word and example to define the role of the modern Latter-day Saint woman. She said, particularly before gatherings of women, that women and men have equal responsibility to gain faith and live righteously. Women by nature must be the mothers and by preference should engage in nurturing. But being a mother and homemaker is not a menial job; it is the most challenging of all occupations, calling for the best preparation and effort. Education serves two ends: it prepares for marriage and it prepares for employment. Most women will for at least part of their life need to work in the labor force, and many women will of necessity spend their whole life working outside the home.

Whether at home or at work, she taught, women as well as men need to perfect themselves by adherence to two great, broad principles — love and service. Our development into Christ-like persons is our individual responsibility. Our happiness is largely in our own hands. And as we love and serve one another, in family, church, community, and world, we help prepare the world for the coming of Zion, a true community of saints.

These are her messages, here represented in several complete talks and articles and in edited excerpts from other talks, interviews, and journals.* There are few enough women whose words are available to us; it is because of both her position and her personality that she is one of those few. May this collection honor her memory by proving useful.

Acknowledgments

I express appreciation to Ardeth Greene Kapp and Carolyn Rasmus for suggesting this book and offering continuing encouragement; to Carolyn Cannon and Cherie Murray for typing assistance; to Eleanor Knowles for careful editing; and to Bee Kimball for her advice and patience.

Royalties from this publication go to the Camilla Eyring Kimball Scholarship Fund at Brigham Young University.

---

*Another address, titled "Women of Faith," appears in *A Heritage of Faith* (Deseret Book, 1988). Additional information is available in the biographies *Camilla* (Deseret Book, 1980) and *Spencer W. Kimball* (Bookcraft, 1977) and a videotape, "Conversations with Camilla."

TALKS AND ARTICLES

1

Keys for a Woman's Progression

Brigham Young University, February 3, 1977

I first came to Provo sixty-five years ago, a frightened, bewildered refugee. My family had lived in Colonia Juarez, Mexico, and was forced to leave in 1912 when revolutionaries in the Mexican civil war threatened the Mormon colonies in Chihuahua and Sonora. I was seventeen when we fled by train to El Paso, Texas, leaving practically everything behind. I recall one of the revolutionaries brazenly lifting a woman's purse from her arm with the barrel of his rifle as she boarded the train.

It was a traumatic experience for us all to leave our homes and start again in a new country. For a few days we were housed in stalls in a lumberyard in El Paso. The curious came to stare at us. Finally Father came out of Mexico on horseback, and we rented some rooms. My uncle Carl Eyring

3

was in Provo, Utah, attending Brigham Young University along with his sister. They wrote, inviting me to come live with them and finish high school at BYU. This was most generous of them, for they were hard-pressed for funds enough to keep the two of them in school.

The next two years at BYU left me with indelible memories. They were hard, poverty-ridden years, but a time of great personal growth. I learned and prepared myself for employment as a teacher of home economics in the Church academies. I came to love BYU, and through the years I have watched with a thrill as this school has grown tremendously in size and in worldwide influence. I read the school papers and envy you the many wonderful cultural and intellectual opportunities. I have thought that when my husband and I get to retirement age, perhaps we can come to Provo and be active participants in the wonderful programs available here. I hope each of you has some sense of what a great privilege it is to be part of this institution and that you make every day count in learning and in making lasting friendships.

I appreciate this invitation to be with you at the beginning of this conference and share some ideas of how women can best fulfill their calling in life.

Spiritual Growth

The Lord expects men and women alike, first of all, to grow in spirituality—that is, to worship him; to gain understanding of the kind of being he is and wants us to become; to develop deep, abiding faith; and to live by divine principles of conduct. No other school in the whole world is so richly endowed with the resources to teach the whole truth—to teach the important, eternal verities as well as the worldly knowledge we need for vocation and for enjoyment of life. Of all we learn in life, the single most important knowledge we can attain is a firm testimony of the Lord Jesus Christ as our Savior and an understanding of the path he would have us follow.

Sometimes we are accused of being boastful in declaring that we belong to the only true church. But we say it not in pride but in gratitude, considering ourselves blessed to have been born members of the Church or to have had favorable opportunity to hear the gospel preached so that we would understand and accept it. We reject no truth or good to be found anywhere, but are anxious to share that added truth which we have. All truth is a part of the gospel. Truth is things as they were, as they are, and as they will be. We are not so arrogant as to assert that the Church's programs are perfect, for the Church continues to add programs to meet the changing times, nor would we say that its members are perfect. We have a long way to go before we have become all that the Lord wants us to be. But we do say to all who will listen, "Here is more truth than can be found anywhere else in this world, because God has established his church to teach his children as much as is within their present capacity to learn," and we say to others, "Come and share with us!"

Many years ago, when we were vacationing in Long Beach, California, I went to the public library to look for books to read. As I browsed through the shelves, a strange woman came up beside me and, with no preliminary introduction, said to me in a demanding voice, "Are you saved?" Taken aback, I paused a second to consider. Then I answered, "Well, I'm working on it." With firm conviction, she admonished, "You'd better accept Christ now and be saved, or you may be too late!" I have thought about this encounter many times since, and my answer to the question would of necessity still be the same today: "I'm working on it." Of course, our salvation depends upon our acceptance of Christ, but also on our continual progress and our remaining faithful to the end. Salvation is a process, not an event. A major part of that process is in service. King Benjamin said, "When ye are in the service of your fellow beings ye are only in the service of your God." (Mosiah 2:17.)

Service to Our Families

What shall we serve? Our first obligation is to our families. So far as we know, the Church organization may not be found in heaven, but families will be. God joined Adam and Eve in the holy bonds of marriage even before they were mortal, and commanded them to cleave to one another. God has through all ages fostered the family, giving to mankind the sealing power so that families can be joined for eternity. The importance of our finding worthy companions and of temple marriage cannot be overestimated when we realize that our eternal destiny depends in part upon this sacred ordinance. Without it, we cannot have fullness of joy. With it, the future is boundless. There are some who, through no fault of their own, do not have that opportunity in this life, but as President Harold B. Lee said, "No one worthy of these blessings will be denied them indefinitely." Life stretches beyond mortality, and those who live worthily will find fulfillment in the hereafter.

As husbands and wives, parents and children, our foremost duty and opportunity of service is to one another. President David O. McKay said that "no other success can compensate for failure in the home." We must take advantage of every effective means to strengthen home ties.

The family home evening program has long been a part of the Church plan. I remember well as a child the occasions in our family when we gathered together and each child, beginning with the youngest, had a part on the home evening program. These are happy memories. When my brothers and sisters get together even now, we often reminisce about those times, repeating with laughter the poems and songs we performed back in those days.

It was fun to hear my brother Henry sing in monotone, "What can little bodies do? / Like us little lispers, / Full of life and mischief, too, / And prone to noisy whispers." And Joe's oft-repeated contribution as a little three-year-old was,

"Three little rabbits went out to run, / Uphill and downhill, / Oh, what fun!"

The songs the family sang together are still our favorites. Some of them were folk songs brought from England by our great-grandmother. We still sing these with our grandchildren, and these are traditions that bind the family together.

In recent years more definite and concerted effort is being made to perfect the program. We have come to realize that Monday family home evening should be as regular and important a part of our lives as attendance at sacrament meeting—that it is worth sacrifices to keep this time special for those close to us.

Many people outside the Church are recognizing and adopting the family home evening as a tool to strengthen their families. Recently my husband spoke at a convention of young business executives and their wives at Sun Valley, Idaho. None of them were members of the Church, but several of them came personally to express appreciation for our family home evening manual, which they were using with their families.

A first major effort by the Church to reach the world with this message, the recent nationwide television program on home evening, has had much greater response than anticipated. Thousands of requests for the home evening booklet have been received from all parts of the country. What a chance, by precept and example, to have important impact on the lives of our neighbors!

We are by no means the only ones to recognize the importance of the family. Dr. Earl Schaefer at the University of North Carolina has affirmed that "parents and the home environment are more critical to a child's educational success than schools and teachers are." Three years of research has produced "a tremendous amount of evidence that parents' involvement with the child has the greatest impact in achievement, in curiosity, persistence—even creativity." It has long been said that children whose parents have read aloud to them learn to read better and with greater enjoyment than children who do not have such experience. Also, those coming from homes where books are read, ideas discussed, and art appreciated prove to be better students than those who miss these experiences.

I am sure most of us could bear testimony to the value of our home environment, where family ideals were inculcated in us that have provided lasting guidelines for our lives.

Young people anticipating marriage and family should keep these findings firmly in mind. Mothers with small children cannot overestimate the importance of the mother's place in the home with her children. Whoever shares that time with the children will largely determine their character and shape their lives. What a challenge for women!

I still have a vivid memory of my mother sitting at the table after supper in the evening with the lighted coal-oil lamp and an open book before her. As she read aloud to us, she at the same time was knitting stockings for the family. The click of the knitting needles punctuated the stories she read. From her example I learned to love books and to reject idleness.

Good books were always an important part of our home life. I remember, though, one day when I was small and came home from the library with the book *Camille* by Emile Zola, anticipating reading it because the title of the book was so much like my name. The minute Mama saw the book, she exclaimed, "Oh, no, dear, you don't want to read that book!" She promptly returned it to the library. A good many years later I read it and then realized that she was quite right in thinking I was much too young for it the first time. I am grateful that she loved me enough to establish standards in our home. The existence of reasonable rules is almost as important as their content.

From a magazine article, "A Child Needs Love," by Rita Chapman of Dallas, Texas, I quote:

I am totally convinced that once a woman has borne a child, she owes that child herself more than anything else in the first five years of his life. . . .

I fear that raising emotion-starved and love-starved children can produce calloused, robotized adults—people who follow the group in straight lines and do exactly what everyone else is doing, because someone has said it is time.

I fear for the working mother who is deluded to believe that some kind, patient woman will tend to her child's emotional needs until she can take over, that someone else will see that her child discovers he is unique, until she can pick him up at the end of the day—when she is perhaps so tired that the best he can hope to hear is, "It's time to go to bed."

I fear for the future of the child whose hunger for love and recognition must be satisfied in large groups. I beg mothers to wake up, to experience the precious dawning of their child's life with him. Evening comes quickly—but in the evening may be too late. (Quoted in *Church News*, August 14, 1976.)

The impact of what parents do in the home extends beyond the home, to community and nation. Michael Novak, in *Harper's* magazine, said:

Throughout history, nations have been able to survive a multi-plicity of disasters—invasions, famines, earthquakes, epidemics, depressions, but they have never been able to survive the disinte-gration of the family. The family is the seed bed of economic skills, money habits, attitude toward work, and the art of financial inde-pendence. It is a stronger agency of education than the school and stronger for religious training than the church. What strengthens the family strengthens the society; . . . if things go well with the family, life is worth living. When the family falters, life falls apart. ("Family Out of Favor," *Harper's* 252 [April 1976]: 37-40.)

We are in a period when the great propaganda machines are telling us that for a woman to choose a career in home and family is somehow demeaning, and that self-respect demands that she pursue a profession of law or medicine or business. But rather than directing both marriage partners away from the home, we need to encourage both to make the strengthening of the family their primary concern. There is challenge, accomplishment, and satisfaction enough for anyone in this greatest educational endeavor — the home.

Service to Fellow Church Members

In the rural society of my childhood, we often lived close enough to grandparents, uncles and aunts, brothers and sisters, and cousins to use their physical and psychic resources to supplement our own. When we needed help, they were there. But in our highly mobile society today, this extended family is rarely so available. And today fellow Church members often fill that function. The visiting teaching and home teaching programs can provide support of this kind. Every family in the Church has two pairs of teachers who, taken together, should visit that home at least two dozen times a year with a spiritual message and a constant reminder that others care for us. We are responsible for one another. I help you and you help me. These visiting programs offer some of the strongest evidence that we are truly willing to serve one another and that the Church is an extension of the family idea.

In the Church organization, there are ample opportunities for both men and women. I have felt no deprivation in not holding the priesthood. I feel only gratitude that I can, with my husband and sons, receive all its blessings without my having to assume many of its responsibilities. I have had teaching and leadership positions enough to give me full range for my abilities. In my fifty years as a visiting teacher of the Relief Society, I have had some of my richest human and spiritual experiences. In times of sickness and sorrow, there are very specific needs. In other homes you may be the only contact an inactive family has with the Church. The hand of friendship and fellowship is often the means of reactivation of these families.

It is clear to me that from an eternal perspective it does not matter where we serve but only how faithfully we serve. To each person who has a calling as a teacher of families in the Church, I say be faithful and supportive, fulfilling that responsibility to the best of your abilities. And to each of us who is in a family being taught, I say let us make our teachers welcome and allow them to serve us, for in so doing we both shall be blessed.

The Pursuit of Knowledge

If we want to give effective service to our families and our neighbors, as we are commanded to do, we must develop ourselves to our full potential. We need to enlarge our intellect and perfect our character. We need to become more Christ-like.

The pursuit of knowledge, which is characteristic of a university, is not only permissible — it is part of the gospel plan for us. The revelation given through the Prophet Joseph Smith in section 88 of the Doctrine and Covenants sets the scope of our study:

Teach ye diligently and my grace shall attend you, that you may be instructed more perfectly in theory, in principle, in doctrine, in the law of the gospel, in all things that pertain unto the kingdom of God, that are expedient for you to understand;

Of things both in heaven and in the earth, and under the earth; things which have been, things which are, things which must shortly come to pass; things which are at home, things which are abroad; the wars and the perplexities of the nations, and the judgments which are on the land; and a knowledge also of countries and of kingdoms —

That ye may be prepared in all things when I shall send you again to magnify the calling whereunto I have called you, and the mission with which I have commissioned you. . . .

And as all have not faith, seek ye diligently and teach one another words of wisdom; yea, seek ye out of the best books words of wisdom; seek learning, even by study and also by faith. (D&C 88:78-80, 118.)

My feeling is that each of us has the potential for special accomplishment in some field. The opportunities for women

to excel are greater today than ever before. We should all
be resourceful and ambitious, expanding our interests. Forget self-pity and look for mountains to climb. Everyone has
problems. The challenge is to cope with those problems
and get our full measure of joy from life. These "words of
wisdom" from books are a means to that end.

Here and now you are much engrossed in textbooks,
which are often tedious but important to the task of preparing
for a specific career. They are keys that open doors, windows
that open on life.

Some of the delightful pleasures of life are in continuing
education in our mature years and in collecting and reading
fine books. Continue to pick up interesting information in
history, current events, the arts. There are various areas that
we may miss in the few years we are enrolled in college,
and learning confined to four years is soon out of date.

Through the years I have found it stimulating to be enrolled in a college class or two each year. The stimulation
of association with young people helps keep one alive. For
some years in Arizona I worked in the city library, which
was sponsored by the Federated Women's Club. I helped in
the selection of books and found this a challenge to keep
up with current literature. I still belong to one or another
of the book clubs that bring a variety of reading material
into our home, and I make a concerted effort to select worthwhile books.

And beyond books, learning means keeping the mind
open to all kinds of experiences. Travel when you have a
chance. Travel with an open mind, an alert eye, and a wish
to understand other people, other places. That fits us all the
better for most of life's callings.

When our children were young, every summer we, with
them, made a trip by car to visit the different areas of America,
east, west, north, and south. This way we gained a greater
appreciation for our great country. Going to Rotary International conventions, especially to Mexico and Europe,

broadened our outlook. We worked at touring, seeing countries and people in detail.

For the past thirty-three years it has been my privilege, with my husband, to visit the members of the Church in countries all around the world. This has been an opportunity to get close to the people, to feel their needs. The first fundamental need of every person is the indispensability of love to every human being, the feeling of being of value to others.

Our interdependence with others is the most encompassing fact of human reality. We need each other.

An Integrated Personality

Much unhappiness has been suffered by those people who have never recognized that it is as necessary to make themselves into whole and harmonious personalities as to keep themselves clean, healthy, and financially solvent. Wholeness of the mind and spirit is not a quality conferred by nature or by God. It is like health and knowledge. We all have the capacity to attain it, but to achieve it depends on our own efforts. It needs a long, deliberate effort of the mind and the emotions and even the body. During our earthly life the body gradually slows down, but the mind has the capacity to grow even more lively and active. The chief limitations confronting us are not age or sex or race or money. Those who avoid learning or abandon it find that life becomes dry, but when the mind is alert, life is luxuriant. No learner has ever run short of subjects to explore. You can live most rewardingly by attaining and preserving the joy of learning and serving.

Let me say in summary that with all the other knowledge that enriches our lives, we must not forget to include the knowledge of the gospel of Jesus Christ. When we think how fervently earthly parents want their children to grow up in faithfulness, we can appreciate in some small measure the great desire our Heavenly Father has that his beloved children may find their way back to him. Living the gospel is not the easiest way of life, but it is the most rewarding way.

I am grateful for the understanding we have of our responsibility to become God-like in character, to love our children and neighbors as he loves us. The family is important enough to call for our best efforts — no profession is more noble than homemaking. The fullness of respect from good people and from God comes to those who fit themselves to serve and then serve one another — and family first of all — with love.

I am grateful for the example set by Christ and for his great atoning sacrifice. I know that he lives. My prayer for us all is that we may follow his admonition to seek divine perfection in our lives and endure faithful and joyful to the end of our lives so that we may worthily claim our reward in his kingdom.

2

The Rewards of Correct Choices

Brigham Young University, February 7, 1981

I am pleased to meet with so many of you who are here to participate in this women's conference. It is a marvelous opportunity to exchange ideas. It serves to remind us of the wide range of choices we make in life and the importance of choosing well.

It has been a circuitous path that brings me back to BYU again sixty-eight years after I first arrived here as a frightened seventeen-year-old refugee from the revolution in Mexico. That was a major step in the great lifelong adventure in education I have enjoyed, an adventure that continues today as much as ever. I have always reserved a special place in my heart for this school, though it bears scant resemblance today to the little academy I came to in 1912. I imagine that date sounds like prehistoric time to you young people.

Actually, I have lived from the days of the horse and buggy to the age of the jet plane. When I was a little girl we lived in the village of Colonia Juarez, Mexico. My grandmother Romney lived eighteen miles away in Colonia Dublan. Once a month the family made the trip so my mother could visit her mother. There was one special trip we made in the buggy with a special team of horses Papa had purchased. We boasted about making this trip in the unheard-of space of three hours. By contrast, just a few months ago my husband and I flew in a jet from New York City to London in three hours and twenty-nine minutes. That seems almost impossible.

The theme of this conference, as you have been reminded several times, is from the second book of Nephi. May I review with you its context.

Lehi and his fractious band had been led by God out of Palestine across the sea to a new land. Not many generations had been born when Jacob, ordained to be teacher of his people, delivered a great sermon in which he summarized the message of redemption he had been preaching for many years. One gets the impression that he was speaking to a somewhat discouraged people. He reviewed at length the Lord's great covenants with the house of Israel, to which the Nephites belonged, and reminded them that in due time the Lord would take upon himself flesh and would suffer and die for all men. He then concluded his teaching for the day and promised to continue the next day.

When the Nephites gathered again, Jacob told them of an angelic visitation he had received during the night. In that revelation additional information was given to him regarding the earthly ministry of the Christ, and he was told again that the land to which they had been led had been set aside as an inheritance for the peoples who had been led there. Jacob, in seeking to comfort this band of people cut off from their homeland, reminded them that the Lord was continually mindful of them in their exile, and that wherever they might be and whatever their circumstances, their personal struggle for salvation must go on just the same. He said, "Therefore, cheer up our hearts, and remember that ye are free to act for yourselves — to choose the way of everlasting death or the way of eternal life. Wherefore, my beloved brethren, reconcile yourselves to the will of God, and not to the will of the devil and the flesh." (2 Nephi 10:23-24.)

Nephi was highly selective in the portions of Jacob's sermon he recorded, so he must have considered this passage to be important. It states a fundamental principle of the gospel: that we are free to choose. We call this principle free will or free agency. I have thought about the concept of free agency, and it has seemed to me to have four components: (1) the existence of alternatives; (2) knowledge of those alternatives; (3) the ability to choose from among the alternatives; and (4) responsibility for the choice made.

The Need for Alternatives

First, then, there must be alternatives or contrast or opposition. No passage of scripture is more explicit on this issue than Lehi's great discourse to his son Jacob:

For it must needs be, that there is an opposition in all things. If not so, my first-born in the wilderness, righteousness could not be brought to pass, neither wickedness, neither holiness nor misery, neither good nor bad. Wherefore, all things must needs be a compound in one; wherefore, if it should be one body it must needs remain as dead, having no life neither death, nor corruption nor incorruption, happiness nor misery, neither sense nor insensibility.

Wherefore, it must needs have been created for a thing of naught; wherefore there would have been no purpose in the end of its creation. Wherefore, this thing must needs destroy the wisdom of God and his eternal purposes, and also the power, and the mercy, and the justice of God. (2 Nephi 2:11-12.)

John the Revelator expressed a similar divine disdain for blandness, quoting the Spirit as saying of the Church in

Laodicea, "I know thy works, that thou art neither cold nor hot; I would thou wert cold or hot. So then because thou art lukewarm, and neither cold nor hot, I will spue thee out of my mouth." (Revelation 3:15-16.)

Freedom to choose presupposes the existence of alternatives. Change and contrast and opposition give vitality to life. Even sin and rebellion serve a function. The futility of existence without contrast, without sin, is underscored in Lehi's explanation of the Fall:

> If Adam had not transgressed . . . all things which were created must have remained in the same state in which they were after they were created; and they must have remained forever, and had no end.
>
> And they would have . . . remained in a state of innocence, having no joy, for they knew no misery; doing no good, for they knew no sin.
>
> But behold, all things have been done in the wisdom of him who knoweth all things.
>
> Adam fell that men might be; and men are, that they might have joy.
>
> And the Messiah cometh in the fulness of time, that he may redeem the children of men from the fall. And because that they are redeemed from the fall they become free forever, knowing good from evil; to act for themselves and not to be acted upon, . . . free to choose liberty and eternal life . . . or to choose captivity and death. (2 Nephi 2:22-27.)

We have learned that when astronauts remain in space a long time, they lose mineralization in their bones; and unless they guard against it, weightlessness can also affect their hearts and other muscles enough to make them unfit when they return to an environment where gravity exerts its constant pull. Likewise, we are inclined to long for ease in our lives, but it is a common observation that those who struggle and overcome are the ones who have the greatest satisfaction.

The passage from the Revelation of John decrying lukewarmness continues in this vein: "I counsel thee to buy of me gold tried in the fire, that thou mayest be rich. . . . As many as I love, I rebuke and chasten; be zealous therefore, and repent. . . . He that hath an ear, let him hear." (Revelation 3:18-19, 22.)

Knowledge of Alternatives

If the first requisite of free agency is the existence of alternatives, the second is knowledge of those alternatives. If we are afloat on the sea, out of sight of land, and if there is one direction that will soonest bring us to safe harbor but we have no way of ascertaining that direction, we cannot fairly be judged good or bad sailors for picking whatever course chance gives us.

The scriptures remind us over and over again that without knowledge, there is not full moral responsibility. Paul wrote, "For there is no respect of persons with God. For as many as have sinned without law shall also perish without law." (Romans 2:11-12.) And Jacob taught the Lehites:

> Where there is no law given there is no punishment; and where there is no punishment there is no condemnation; and where there is no condemnation the mercies of the Holy One of Israel have claim upon them, because . . . the atonement satisfieth the demands of his justice upon all those who have not the law given to them . . . and they are restored to that God who gave them breath. . . . But wo unto him that has . . . all the commandments of God, like unto us, and that transgresseth them, and that wasteth the days of his probation, for awful is his state. (2 Nephi 9:25-27.)

The prime example of one who stands innocent because he lacks knowledge is the child. The rest of us will come sooner or later to knowledge. King Benjamin said: "The time shall come when the knowledge of a Savior shall spread throughout every nation. . . . And behold, when that time cometh, none shall be found blameless before God, except it be little children." (Mosiah 3:20-21.)

Awareness of alternatives is important, but sometimes it may be too much to speak of knowledge. Often we must walk by faith, not discerning the choices clearly. Good and evil, black and white, and right and wrong are the simple cases, the extremes. Nearer the middle, it is difficult to distinguish boundaries. If the light is dim, we should seek more light, but ultimately we must make our choices with whatever light we have received.

Choosing from Among the Alternatives

The third component of free agency is to choose from among the alternatives we know. Choice in life is not just an occasional thing. We are afloat on a sea of choices. And we ought not to think that we can avoid accountability by refusing to make a choice, because refusing to decide is itself a choice—a choice to be borne wherever external forces will take us.

Choice has meaning only with reference to real alternatives. We are not wholly independent of circumstances; wind and tide and current all have their influence. We can choose the direction of our striving and head for whatever shore we wish, but we may be driven back like the Arctic explorer who struggled all day on pack ice toward the North Pole only to find that the current had moved him back farther than where he had started. We may wonder at strong forces that seem to overwhelm our poor powers of choice, but it is part of our faith that in matters of eternal importance our destiny is indeed in our hands.

Free agency does not mean that all possibilities are open to us. One cannot choose to be younger or more beautiful, to know what is unknowable, or to be successful or loved. A person can choose to do things that may tend to bring about some of those conditions, but a person's ultimate achievement is outside individual control. Happily, we understand, the judgment of God is to be based largely on what we have done with the choices open to us—not on absolute results, but on progress. We are responsible for direction and effort.

Once we understand the options actually open to us, it still takes courage to choose rightly. And sometimes we need to be reminded over and over again. Joshua, aging and seeing the children of Israel beginning to stray again after the strange gods of their neighbors, called his people together to elicit from them one last commitment before he died. First, he reminded them of how the Lord had fought their battles when they came to occupy the Promised Land. He said, speaking for God, "I have given you a land for which ye did not labour, and cities which ye built not, and . . . vineyards . . . which ye planted not." Joshua then challenged them: "Now therefore fear the Lord, and serve him in sincerity and in truth; and put away the gods which your fathers served. . . . Choose you this day whom ye will serve . . . : but as for me and my house, we will serve the Lord."

The people responded, "Therefore will we also serve the Lord."

But Joshua prodded, "He will not forgive your transgressions . . . if ye forsake the Lord, and serve strange gods."

The people said, "Nay; but we will serve the Lord."

And Joshua said, "Ye are witnesses against yourselves that ye have chosen you the Lord, to serve him."

And they replied, "We are witnesses."

Joshua persisted, "Now therefore put away . . . the strange gods which are among you and incline your heart unto the Lord God of Israel."

The people chorused, "The Lord our God will we serve, and his voice will we obey." (See Joshua 24:13-24.)

You see how Joshua, in drawing out those audience responses, worked at getting his people to make a choice and then to repeat it and reaffirm it. He then set up a great stone as a memorial of their promise, to stand as a permanent witness to their covenant. And we should remember that gospel ordinances are designed to remind us again and again of our commitments.

Having to choose is every person's lot. Even those great and good spirits whom God chose in the premortal existence to be his rulers had to undergo the same testing process. Alma speaks of the high priests who were "called and prepared from the foundation of the world according to the foreknowledge of God, on account of their exceeding faith and good works," but he notes that they were "in the first place . . . left to choose good or evil; therefore they having chosen good, and exercising exceeding great faith, are called with a holy calling." Others who were on the same standing with their brethren "might have had as great privilege," but they "would reject the Spirit of God on account of the hardness of their hearts and blindness of their minds." (See Alma 13:1-4.)

Sometimes the results of our choices come promptly, but often outcomes are long delayed so that our knowledge is only tentative and is based upon what we are told by spokesmen we believe and upon extension of our past experience. It is part of the Lord's plan that we see through the glass only darkly for the most part (1 Corinthians 13:12), and that there be trial of our faith. The Lord said, through Brigham Young, "My people must be tried in all things, that they may be prepared to receive the glory that I have for them, even the glory of Zion; and he that will not bear chastisement is not worthy of my kingdom." (D&C 136:31.) These factors make our choosing more difficult and stressful.

Sometimes we feel nearly overwhelmed and would like to deny responsibility for our decisions, but we are taught that we may not do so. Joseph Smith said that "the devil has no power over us only as we permit him." (*Teachings of the Prophet Joseph Smith*, comp. Joseph Fielding Smith [Salt Lake City: Deseret Book Co., 1938], p. 181.) The same principle is expressed by Paul: "God . . . will not suffer you to be tempted above that ye are able; but will with the temptation also make a way to escape, that ye may be able to bear it." (1 Corinthians 10:13.)

Responsibility for Our Choices

The final component of free agency is that we bear responsibility for our choices. Samuel the Lamanite said on this subject: "Remember, my brethren, that whosoever perisheth, perisheth unto himself; . . . for behold, ye are . . . permitted to act for yourselves; . . . God hath given unto you a knowledge and he hath made you free." (Helaman 14:30.) Once we make an understanding choice among alternatives, we have responsibility for each choice poorly made and can expect rich reward for each choice made wisely.

Our accountability is individual. As Ezekiel says, "The son shall not bear the iniquity of the father, neither shall the father bear the iniquity of the son: the righteousness of the righteous shall be upon him, and the wickedness of the wicked shall be upon him." (Ezekiel 18:20.) And it is not only the momentous decisions that we must account for. The Savior taught, "Every idle word that men shall speak, they shall give account thereof in the day of judgment." (Matthew 12:36.) As Alma said, "If we have hardened our hearts against the word, . . . our words will condemn us, yea, all our works will condemn us; . . . and our thoughts will also condemn us." (Alma 12:13-14.)

Rewards for correct choices come in all shapes and sizes, large and small, but none are insignificant. Blessings come by obedience: "When we obtain any blessing from God, it is by obedience to that law upon which it is predicated." (D&C 130:21.)

If we avoid harmful drugs and eat wholesome foods, we are promised improved health, hidden treasures of knowledge, stamina, and protection from the destroying angel. (See D&C 89.)

If we bring our tithes and offerings into the Lord's storehouse, he will open the windows of heaven to pour out overflowing blessings; he will protect our crops and will make our land delightsome. (See Malachi 3:8-10.)

If we keep a personal journal, we can expect to be held in honorable memory by our descendants, who will learn from our experiences and testimony.

If we love one another, Christ will love us. If we are his disciples, he will call us his friends. (See John 15:10-14.)

If we observe the Lord's day, confessing, fasting, and praying, and doing so cheerfully, the fullness of the earth is ours. (See D&C 59:9-16.)

If we render service to one another, trying to repay our Father, we can never catch up because he will shower us with more blessings. (See Mosiah 2:20-22.)

In a hundred other ways our choice to obey the Lord will help us reap rich rewards.

There is one reward, above all else, that we may hope for. That reward is exaltation. The Lord gives us the free gift of resurrection, even if we have made wrong choices, but we can partake fully of his atoning sacrifice only if we meet his conditions. The passage from which our theme is taken admonishes us: "Reconcile yourselves to the will of God . . . and remember . . . that it is only in and through the grace of God that ye are saved. Wherefore, may God raise you from death by the power of the resurrection, and also from everlasting death by the power of the atonement, that ye may be received into the eternal kingdom of God, that ye may praise him through grace divine." (2 Nephi 10:24-25.) We are told further that if we make the eternal marriage covenant through the priesthood power and abide in that covenant, we shall pass to exaltation and glory and a continuation of the seeds forever and be gods from everlasting to everlasting, joining Abraham, Isaac, and Jacob in that blessed condition. (See D&C 132:19-20, 37.)

Many of the rewards, however certain, are far in the future. It requires faith to endure to the end when the rewards seem so long delayed. It is as with the Lord's coming: some will give up in despair; others will still be prepared, their lamps having been filled with oil. When he came the first time, many had given up their faith that the sign Samuel the Lamanite had predicted would mark Christ's birth would actually occur. They thought the time was past. But the faithful, despite threats of imminent death, remained steadfast, knowing in whom they trusted.

In an ultimate sense, of course, we cannot earn salvation by our wise choices or our good deeds. We do what we can, but the goal is far beyond us. Someone else must bridge the chasm, "for we know that it is by grace that we are saved, after all we can do." (2 Nephi 25:23.)

Jesus reminded his disciples, "Ye have not chosen me, but I have chosen you." (John 15:16.) We seek to follow the Savior, adhering to his teachings, emulating his virtues, enduring whatever burdens may be placed upon us, bearing his name, accepting his great sacrifice, and calling upon his grace. We then have to hope that he will reach out and draw us to him, making us more than we have made ourselves.

We Are Free and Responsible

I have tried to take you with me, through my reading and thinking about this great principle of the gospel, to the idea that we are both free and responsible. On the one hand, it helps me to be more diligent if I can see my place in the larger scheme of things and if I can be reminded what glorious things await us. But on the other hand, there is often so great a gap between our hope of heaven and the daily round of mundane activities that I must struggle to keep them in eternal perspective. I learn great principles best in simple applications.

I can see clearly that my earthly life has been greatly affected by choices I have made along the way. My choice of friends has helped keep me straight. I have had friends who expected me to be good, and I have tried not to disappoint them.

My choice to obey my parents had the same effect. I recall my first real date to a dance. I had accepted the invitation from a boy before I talked to my parents. My father objected to the boy. My tears got me permission to go with him just that once, but I did not go with him again; I did not consider disobeying my father. Though I did not always understand or agree with his judgment, I knew he had my welfare at heart. Several years later, when I began going with Spencer Kimball, my father had no objection. He recognized him as a man of quality.

It is obvious how much the direction of my life has been affected by my choice of a husband. On the eve of our wedding I shed a great many tears over the uncertainty caused by the prospect of his having to go off to war, over giving up the plans I had made for a profession, and over the magnitude of the commitment I was making. But I knew that he was a faithful, energetic, capable person and that I loved him very much. I believed that together we could have a happy life and move step by step toward returning, with our family, to our Father in heaven. Choosing that road has made all the difference.

My decision to pursue an education and become a teacher gave me some skills I could put to use in the family and in the Church and community. Because I chose to read for pleasure, I ended up with an activity that has enriched my life greatly and has helped me motivated my children to love learning. For some time I was the volunteer librarian in our small-town library in Arizona, and that gave me the opportunity to select the books that would go on its shelves.

I made the less-than-wise choice as a young mother when I became deeply engrossed in playing bridge. I played several afternoons a week and enjoyed it immensely. Then Elder Melvin J. Ballard came to stake conference and called upon us to put aside our bridge games. At first I rebelled; then I acquiesced, finally realizing how much I could better use that time I had been giving up to the game. It was a test of obedience. I chose to obey.

I make no pretensions at perfection. People sometimes assume that because I am the President's wife I must already have arrived at that state, but I struggle every day with the same kinds of imperfections you all do. There is no place so high that it is beyond difficulty or temptation. That is part of the human condition. It is a truism that the Lord does not judge us by what we have but by what we do with what we have. The rich may be haughty, the poor envious, the powerful cruel, the weak sniveling. And those between the extremes may well be complacent and lukewarm.

The scriptures remind us that for people "to be learned is good if they hearken unto the counsels of God." (2 Nephi 9:29.) To be rich is good if you can be humble. To be learned is good if you can be wise. To be healthy is good if you can be useful. To be beautiful is good if you can be gracious.

There is, however, nothing inherently bad in being poor, unlettered, sickly, or plain. To be poor is good if you can still be generous of spirit. To be unschooled is good if it motivates you to be curious. To be sickly is good if it helps you to have compassion. To be plain is good if it saves you from vanity.

Every life is full of challenges. I know something of losing one's parents, of seeing one's spouse racked with stress and pain, of having one's savings of many years wiped out by theft or bank failure, of watching loved ones stray from the gospel, of having a child stricken with crippling illness, and of feeling disabling old age creeping on.

Your challenges may be different but no easier. They may involve the high cost of honesty, the impulse of inappropriate sexual involvement, worldly activities that try to crowd out time for prayer and gospel study, disappointment in people you thought you could trust, the collapse of dearly held dreams. Remember that no trial is too great, no task too hard, for you and the Lord together.

I pray for us all that we may measure up to the challenges that come to us. I pray that we will have knowledge and wisdom to make right choices. And I pray that we will accept the great atoning sacrifice of Jesus Christ so that he may draw us up and share with us his great eternal work.

3

A Legacy

Relief Society Legacy Lecture, March 26, 1982

A legacy is something handed down from the past, an inheritance. It may be either tangible or intangible. I own nothing tangible from my great-grandmother Caroline Smith, but I do have as a legacy her wisdom and courage in accepting the gospel. She was born in England in 1820. When she was still young, her parents put her in service to a wealthy family in London. While in that situation, she chanced to hear the gospel and believed what she was taught. When she desired to be baptized, she knew her employers would disapprove and try to stop her, so she bundled up a change of clothing and dropped it out the upstairs window, then slipped away to the place that had been arranged for her baptism. When she returned later, the lady of the house saw Caroline's hair wet and demanded to know where she had been and what she had been doing. Caroline told her that she had joined the Mormons. The lady was mighty upset and made life difficult for her. I honor her for her openness to truth and for her courage to act upon her convictions despite the opposition of others.

My father's father, Henry Eyring, was orphaned in Germany at fifteen and made his way to America with his younger sister when he was eighteen. While living in St. Louis, working for a druggist, he heard about the Mormons. He heard that they were cutthroats, and he was fearful of being on the streets at night. But one time he dared to attend one of the Mormon meetings out of curiosity. He carefully sat next to the door so that at first sign of danger he could escape. Favorably impressed by what he heard, he discovered that a fellow workman was a Mormon who was glad to answer his questions and provide him with literature. After reading everything he could get his hands on and praying for knowledge of the truth, he had a vivid dream in which Elder Erastus Snow commanded him to be baptized by a particular man. Just after his twentieth birthday he was baptized exactly as he dreamed. A few months later he was ordained an elder and sent as a missionary to the Cherokee nation.

He continued as a missionary, working part-time to support himself and with little contact with church headquarters. After three years Grandfather married a part-Indian woman, and they had one child who died in infancy. He and his wife separated after a year and a half because she rejected the Church and was irrationally jealous. Grandfather wrote in his life history:

I had now been about 4½ years on the Cherokee mission and felt somewhat desirous to know when I would be released from my labors. Not being able to hear anything from the presidency of the Church, I called upon the Lord in prayer asking him to reveal to me his mind and will in regard to my remaining longer or going up to Zion. The following dream was given to me in answer to my prayer. I dreamed I had arrived in Salt Lake City and immediately went to President Brigham Young's office where I found him. I said to him, "President Young, I have left my mission, having come of my own accord, but if there is anything wrong in this, I'm willing to return and finish my mission." To this President Young replied, "You've stayed long enough. It's all right." Having had dreams before which were literally fulfilled, I had faith to believe that this also would be and consequently commenced at once to prepare for a start. . . . I enjoyed myself excellently while crossing the plains, walking nearly the whole distance, and I should say with a sweet little German woman who was in the party crossing the plains, and to me it was more like a pleasure trip than a toilsome pilgrimage. I arrive in Salt Lake City August 29th, 1860, and . . . the following day Brother Richey and myself called upon President Young who received us very kindly. I said to him, "President Young, I have come without being sent for. If I have done wrong, I am willing to return and finish my mission." President Young answered, "It's all right. We have been looking for you." Thus my dream was literally fulfilled.

I am grateful for the heritage of a man with enough curiosity to investigate a new idea despite his fears, with enough conviction to stay with his mission even after it seemed he had almost been forgotten, and with enough spirituality to receive divine guidance in what he should do. He later served a second mission to his native Germany and a third one to Mexico in 1887. Concerning his success he wrote, "One man living at Morelos took quite an interest and applied for baptism. Being a drunkard, he soon fell back into his old ways and left the Church. I think I must have converted him, for the Lord never did."

My father, Edward Eyring, served a mission in Germany after he was married. I was two years old and Mother was expecting a second baby. She later wrote of that time:

When papa was on his mission . . . I was so sick that I couldn't throw the bedding across the bed. Papa thought he had arranged so we would have plenty while he was gone. He had rented his two span of mules and wagons and the young man was going to pay an amount weekly. He went off with them and was never seen or heard of after. Papa had debts due to him and expected them to be paid to us, but they were never paid. I worked what I could at sewing, making overalls and sacks for Brother Davis. . . . I rented my bed to two school teachers, and I slept on the floor with the baby, Camilla.

Two of my brothers boarded with me, and . . . they lived almost without anything so I could get along. . . .

I was alone with Camilla and my eleven-year-old sister Ethyl when the baby Mary was born. . . . I gradually came to know that Mary was deaf when pounding a pan or slamming doors near her failed to awaken her. I would not let anyone know of Mary's condition, but carried my sorrow secretly. I feared that Ed would return from his mission if he knew. Finally, Camilla and Mary both took very sick, and I feared they would die. I was sick in bed with nervous prostration. . . . The babies got better but I got worse. I didn't want to live . . . everything looked so black. One night I was numb and could feel nothing. Then the blood started to run from my ears in a hemorrhage. Seven of the elders . . . knelt around the bed and each prayed. . . . I really thought I was going to die. As Brother Ivins was going out of the door, I said, "Brother Ivins, aren't you going to pray for me?" He said, "Why, we have been praying for you," but he laid his hands on my head and from that moment I began to get better.

Father finally returned. He wrote this about what he found:

My wife was very brave, never making a single complaint during my absence. . . . When I arrived home . . . she was just recovering from a severe sickness. Camilla was then a big girl of five years and Mary, whom I had never seen, was two years old. I had not known that Mary had been born deaf. I think I never felt so badly in all my life about anything. Nevertheless, I felt to praise the Lord that all was as well as it was.

I have as my legacy the example of parents who sacrificed much — a father who was willing to leave wife and children to serve a mission and a mother who bore without complaint great poverty and deathly illness and one of the great sorrows of her life in the deafness of her child. She said nothing lest she interfere with the mission to which her beloved husband had been called. During all that time he did not know how she had scrimped and saved to support herself and two children and send him money when the resources he had counted on failed.

My mother left me a legacy of thrift. She had suffered such poverty as a child and in her early married life that she could never waste anything—not a chip of wood or a scrap of material or a bite of food. She saved tens of thousands of pennies by scraping the kettle cleaner than anyone else and repairing clothing others might have thrown away. "Clothes may be old," she said, "but there is no sense in their being ragged." When I was married and she came to visit, she spent all the time patching overalls or darning stockings as we visited together. Her motto was "Waste not, want not."

My mother also left me a legacy of optimism and encouragement. She lavished praise on her children and made them believe they were capable of great things. She made it a point to express appreciation to every performer or speaker. She always spoke in superlatives. Everything was "wonderful." Fault-finding was a grievous sin in her eyes, and she refused to listen to gossip or scandal. She had no patience with lazy people or complainers. She was a doer.

I remember when we children would quarrel a bit and be unkind to one another, Mother would start singing, "Angry words, oh, let them never from the lips unbridled slip." We knew immediately what Mother meant and that we'd better hush up.

Mother died at my home of stomach cancer after a long, painful illness, but she did not complain. When the doctor came in for the last time and asked her how she felt, Mother roused herself enough through the haze of pain and drugs to say, almost inaudibly, one last time, "I'm fine, just fine." I followed the doctor out of the room, and he said in exasperation, "What does that woman mean, 'I'm fine, just fine'!"

It is hard to complain, even when you feel like it, with an example such as that to measure yourself against. I think of her as an angel, really. I just don't know how she ever went through all the vicissitudes that she did in those long-ago days, but she literally never complained.

My father left me, as another part of my heritage, a certain venturesomeness. I am basically shy, but there are some things I dare. I love to travel and see new places and people. Papa expressed his inclination for the unusual in exotic animals. On the farm in Arizona, in addition to the normal farm animals, he had Shetland ponies with a buggy and harness, and ostriches and peacocks. He planted fig trees and pomegranates as well as more common fruits, and he planted peanuts as well as ordinary ground crops. No one else in our community had them. He was not a farmer by choice. He had been happiest when engaged in horse and cattle ranching in Mexico, but when we lost all our property there and he had to return to dirt farming to support his two families, he did not complain. He was like Mother in that respect.

Father also left me his fervent, loving testimony. Once he had a dream, which he described this way:

> I thought I saw children pulling weeds, milking cows, pitching hay, irrigating, and doing many laborious tasks. They sometimes complained a little when they saw their neighbors' children playing and having a good time. I told them that sometime they would thank the Lord for having had useful work to do to keep them out of mischief. Too much pleasure and money are much worse than not enough. It's a fact that some people can't stand too much ease and prosperity. Hard work with faith and prayer is safest for most people. . . . There are heaven and hell, and you can take your choice. The way to hell looks easy, and there is almost no halfway place for those who are born and reared in the Church. You know the Lord sent his Only Begotten Son, Jesus Christ, to establish his church in the meridian of time, that all who would believe and be baptized and keep his commandments should be saved. . . . My dear children, I won't always be with you. The gospel is true. Let us conform to its teachings, that we may all be together in the eternal world.

And that was his great objective and his great testimony, which we heard many times.

A legacy is not something imposed on us. It is made available to us, but we have a choice to either accept it or reject it or ignore it. For example, when our forebears have written their life story for us and thereby preserved in convenient form the significant events of their lives for our enlightenment, we may well leave those books gathering dust on the shelf. Yet, I believe we owe such records a measure of reverence. Family history is a kind of scripture if it records how individuals have dealt with the challenges of life and how God has played a role in their lives. Indeed, the scriptures we have canonized in the Church are in large part histories of families and their dealings with God. Legacies call forth responsibilities. When we have received knowledge of the past, we have obligation to use it, to perpetuate it, and to enlarge it.

I have gratefully received my legacy and have sought to make use of it. I am greatly influenced by the teachings and example of my parents. I would like to be like my parents. I cannot be greater than they, because they were among the best of God's children on this earth, but I want to be enough like them so that I can be with them forever. And often, when I pass the pictures of my father and mother on the dresser in our bedroom, I say, "Oh my, it'll be good to see you, Mother and Dad. I hope it isn't long." I look forward with real anticipation to the time when we shall be reunited. Some days the time seems alluringly short. Other days I count up all the things I still have to do and pray for a little more time.

Having received and used the legacy, my responsibility in part is to pass it on to others. I am grateful for the written record of these lives which my parents and grandparents have made. I have from time to time told my children and grandchildren stories about their ancestors, hoping it would interest them and help turn the children's hearts to their fathers. When my family gets together, we often sing two English ballads that Caroline Smith, the serving girl who crept out of the house to be baptized, brought from England and taught to her children. One of the songs is about a gypsy girl who tells the fortune of a handsome young squire and explains to him that he need look no further for a wife, because she is the one he is to marry. He then takes her home to a mansion as his bride. The other song is "The Mistletoe Bough." A beautiful but foolish bride runs off from a Christmas party to hide in the castle, challenging her young husband to be the first to find her. He looks everywhere frantically but cannot find her. Years later an old chest is found in the castle. When it is opened, a skeleton dressed in a bridal gown is discovered. When the bride hid in the chest it snapped shut, trapping her. There is no great moral to either story, but our singing the obscure songs over and over again has provided one more tie with our past. We never get together in any number that we don't sing these songs. We're anxious that the grandchildren and the great-grandchildren will all know them and realize that these songs belong to their heritage.

We have provided our children with copies of the various family histories and have tried to arrange for all our grand-children to have them too. That does not guarantee that our descendants will appreciate their legacy, but we mean at least to make sure it is available to them. Knowledge of family history and pride in relatives' accomplishments tend to give children a degree of self-confidence and high aspi-rations they might otherwise lack.

My responsibility includes adding to the legacy that I pass on. I must, therefore, add a fresh layer of experience to the family history that is closer in time to my grandchil-dren's lives, with conditions more like those they know and with problems they can more immediately understand. There's a certain charm in the stories from 150 years ago, but they begin to take on almost mythical character and seem less relevant to a person faced with what may seem to be wholly different problems. Analogous but more mod-ern experiences to enrich the fund of examples may be had by our own personal experiences. Our stories are likely to have more effect on the conduct of our descendants than the stories of more remote generations.

One of my experiences, which remains fresh seventy years later, is my family's flight from the Mexican revolution in 1912. I hope my descendants will be more empathic with the plight of refugees because they have read or heard me tell of the terror of flight from dangers and of the humiliation of being dependent upon the charity of others. I know I have felt a special kinship with the Vietnamese refugees we have met.

We were in San Diego a few years ago holding conference, and several Vietnamese refugees who were Church members had just come into Camp Pendleton near San Diego. The stake president asked us if we would like to go hold a meeting with them. I shall never forget the empathy I felt for these people who had left their own country. I kept telling myself that, as refugees, we had had more than they did, because at least we could understand the language. I could hardly keep from crying because I knew how they must feel in having to leave their homes.

I relived my own exodus from Mexico. After civil war had broken out in Mexico, conditions became dangerous for the Mormon colonists who lived there. Father came home one evening in 1912 from a church council meeting to tell us that we must be ready by early morning to leave our home and all our possessions to flee to the United States. We had been bottling blackberries all day, so we hid the hundred quarts of berries under the porch floor. We spent the night hiding things in the attic and under the floors, hoping they would not be found until we could come back in a few weeks. Next morning we took a single trunk for the whole family and drove in our buggy nine miles to the depot, where the refugee train was waiting. A band of guerrillas was lined up at the depot with guns and bayonets. I recall how one of the revolutionaries brazenly lifted a woman's purse from her arm with the barrel of his rifle as she boarded the train.

She dared not say anything. The refugees were women and children and a few old men, crowded into the cars with our baggage and rolls of bedding. The men remained behind to try to protect the property. We were only 150 miles south of the border, but it took all day and all night because in some places the track had been destroyed and repairs must be made. We feared the whole time that roving bands of bandits might stop the train and rob us.

When we arrived at the Rio Grande River and were crossing on the bridge, it was just coming daylight and the American flag was blowing in the wind. A great shout of gratitude came up from the whole trainload of people when we saw the Stars and Stripes. We were grateful for the peace and the security of this free land.

We were all taken to a vacant lumberyard. Each family was given a little section where different lengths of lumber had been stored. We hung up blankets and sheets to make a little screen around that few square feet we would occupy. The people of El Paso were really very kind to us, but their curiosity got the best of them, and they came and peeked through the board fence. I was embarrassed that we were such a curiosity and thought to myself, "We're just monkeys in a cage."

Finally Father came out of Mexico on horseback and we rented some rooms. The troubles persisted, so my family decided to stay in the United States and make a fresh start, having lost everything—home, ranch, cattle, and bottled blackberries.

It can be a blessing for us sometimes to receive a real shake-up and know what other people's sorrow is. When I think my family is having a bad time and a lot of sickness and financial problems, I always look around and say, "My goodness, we're not nearly as bad off as many other people that live close to us." We can always find someone whose cross is heavier than ours. They are standing it, and so can we.

In my effort to record some of my life experiences for the benefit of my family, I have tried to avoid boastfulness. I have tried to show something of my weaknesses, as painful as that sometimes is, so that my descendants may more readily believe that the things I say are true. I hope I've established my veracity by being willing to admit my flaws. My testimony may be more credible and my few successes may seem more significant if I have also described my failures.

The older I grow, the more experience I have, the more grateful I am for the gospel of Jesus Christ. Love and understanding and service are our objectives. I pray that our Heavenly Father may help us to follow his kind commands, that we may as families be all reunited in the eternities.

4

Reminiscings

Relief Society Magazine, July 1961

"A man's real possession is his memory. In nothing else is he rich, in nothing else is he poor." (Alexander Smith.)

The happy life is not ushered in at any age "to the sound of drums and trumpets." It grows upon us year by year, little by little, until at last we realize we have it. You do not *find* the happy life; you *make* it. We are continually being reminded these days that material things do not bring happiness, and yet, if we look about us at the struggle being made to accumulate worldly possessions, we know that few of us will admit that the simple life may bring the greatest peace of mind and real happiness. Far too many homes are filled with anxiety and discontent because of the struggle to accumulate things.

There are advantages in having one's life span from the horse and buggy days to the jet age. It is only by contrast that we can fully appreciate. I find delight in reliving my childhood spent in the days when the family was self-sufficient and the small community was one big family. Let me recount for you the activities of yesterday that will bring memories to many of you and may sound like another world to young women of the present generation. Our social science lessons in Relief Society the past two years were designed to help us to have a more mature sense of values. The mature woman does not hesitate to admit her age, we were taught; so I dare to recall the activities of my childhood, which will definitely date me.

As I enjoy the modern conveniences that make housekeeping comparatively easy, I recall the wood-burning stove in our kitchen, sixty years ago, which called for the gathering of chips to start the fire, chopping the wood, and filling the wood box. We are prone to accept the hot and cold water coming from taps as a matter of course, but in the "good old days," we often dipped the water from the irrigation ditch to do the washing, and a well or a pump in the backyard was the beginning of luxury. Hot water was provided from a reservoir on the back of the kitchen stove or from the teakettle, which always had a way of being empty when hot water was needed most. On Saturday afternoon, the wash boiler or extra kettles were placed on the stove to heat water for the weekly baths so that all the family would be clean for Sunday. The kitchen became the bathroom, and each member of the family took a turn for a scrubbing, sitting in the number-three tub.

Monday was always wash day. Clothes were put to soak the night before. Father would build a fire in the backyard, where the tub of water, resting on a circle of rocks, was heated. The clothes were scrubbed on a washboard and then put in the tub of water on the fire to be boiled. It took me many years in later life to be sure clothes could really be sanitary if they had not been boiled. Then came the rinsing, the bluing, and hanging the clothes on the line to dry in the sun. What a fresh, clean smell clothes thus washed do have!

It was a matter of pride to be the first in the neighborhood to have your white clothes hanging on the line. There was real competition, too, to see whose clothes were the whitest. If they were tattle-tale gray, everyone in the neighborhood knew it, as well as all the passers-by.

Ironing day followed on Tuesday. The flatirons were heated on the kitchen stove. Sometimes the smoke from the fire came through the cracks around the lids of the stove, so one must be sure to wipe the iron carefully before using it. As the iron cooled, it was exchanged for a hot one. Ironing was a long and tiring task, but what can be more satisfying than freshly ironed, starched petticoats, dresses, and shirts? It gives a real sense of accomplishment when it is well done.

A daily chore was cleaning and filling the coal-oil lamps. The wick must be carefully trimmed so that the flame would be straight across. Washing and polishing the lamp chimneys was the hardest job of all. Sometimes I tried to get by with wiping them out with paper, but often this didn't pass inspection, and someone was sure to complain if the light was dim when we sat down to read or study.

Fall housecleaning meant turning the house inside out. The homemade carpets in the parlor and bedrooms were untacked from the floors, hung on the clothesline, and beaten vigorously to get out all the dust. The straw padding was gathered up in tubs and the floor carefully washed; when it was dry, a fresh padding of straw was spread and the carpets replaced, stretched, and tacked. How we loved to walk over the freshly laid carpets and feel and hear the new straw crunch underfoot.

In food preparation, do you ever stop to think how many prepared things you buy from the store in cans, bottles, and packages? None of these were available then. For making bread, we usually obtained yeast from a neighbor. I would carry a cup of sugar or flour in a small bucket and, in exchange, receive a quart of yeast made with hops. It was delicious to drink, and I kept taking sips as I carried it home so that

Mother often exclaimed that there was probably not enough left to raise the dough.

During the summer there was the almost continuous task of bottling fruits, vegetables, and meat. Drying apricots, peaches, and corn took many more hours. A special delicacy was homemade hominy. In the fall when the corn was harvested, we would shell it from the cob. Mother soaked the wood ashes in water to leach out the lye. The corn was then soaked in the lye water until the hull could be rubbed off. Then came repeated washings to get every trace of the lye out. When the hominy was cooked and seasoned with butter, it was delicious.

The fall season brought another happy experience, a trip to the molasses mill to get molasses for a candy pull. I remember one occasion especially well. It was getting late in the evening before the candy was done, so to hasten the process of cooling, we poured the boiling candy into a bucket of cold water to cool it quickly so we could pull it. Each of us reached in for a handful. I was a bit too eager and got my hand under the boiling syrup as it was poured out. I carried the blisters and then scars of a bad burn for a long time.

Milk was not delivered in bottles or purchased from the store in cartons. Herding the cows in the pasture during the summer months was healthy work for the children. Sometimes they weren't as careful as they should have been, and a cow would bloat from eating alfalfa. This called for quick action on the part of farm boys, who knew how to put a gag in her mouth or even to "stick" the cow if she was badly bloated. Morning and evening after the cows were milked, Mother strained the warm milk into broad flat pans and placed them in the pantry for the cream to rise. Churning the cream into butter was sometimes a seemingly endless task, if the cream was too cold or too warm. Washing the butter and molding it into pound molds completed a task that took real skill, if the product was to be of first-class quality. Fresh-churned buttermilk was a valued product of the churning. The pans of clabbered milk were made into mounds of cottage cheese, or sometimes just to put a little sugar on the clabber made a delicacy for some members of the family.

The smell of roasting bran and molasses stirred frequently as it browned in the oven, or left-over pieces of bread toasted a dark brown, are another fond memory. These were steeped with water, strained, and served for breakfast with cream and sugar, much as we prepare Postum today.

Making soap was another of Mother's accomplishments. In the backyard was a huge brass kettle into which all the waste fat from the kitchen and pieces of suet from the butchered beef were placed with water and lye. These were boiled together to the right consistency, determined by testing. When the soap was cooled and hardened, it was cut into squares and put on a board to cure. Soap purchased from the store was a special luxury and used only as a toilet article.

"Ready-made" clothes from the store were unknown to us. Underwear, petticoats, dresses, coats, and shirts were all fashioned by busy hands at home. Carefully washed flour sacks were made into petticoats and panties. Sometimes the name of the milling company wouldn't wash out, so that we might be labeled across the back. Father's worn-out suits were carefully washed and turned to make trousers for the boys. There was always a basket of stockings to darn. This was something Mother was especially careful about. No one was ever allowed to wear stockings or clothes that needed mending.

Mother was skilled at knitting, and I can still hear the click of the knitting needles as she knitted stockings for the family. This was her recreation, for she could read as she knit. Hand-knit wool stockings were a great trial to me, for they made my legs itch unmercifully. Father, on the other hand, felt that he couldn't wear any socks except the wool ones Mother knitted. Besides the stockings, she knit many yards of beautiful lace for pillowslips and aprons.

Piecing and making quilts were other never-finished jobs. Mother took the wool, which had been sheared and soaked and washed out. We children had the task of "picking" or loosening the matted fibers. Then Mother would card it into numerous small batts, which she used for the filling of the quilts. When the quilt was ready on the frames, friends and relatives came for an all-day quilting bee. This was a real social occasion and a chance for a good visit.

All worn-out clothing was carefully washed, then torn or cut into short or long strips about an inch wide. These strips were sewed together in hit-and-miss color combinations and then wound into big balls. The balls were stored in the closet until enough accumulated to have a new rag carpet or smaller rugs woven on the hand loom.

Transportation was slow, but it was fun. There were always horses or burros to ride. Young people loved to go for hayrack rides in the moonlight, singing as they rode. Father had a span of extra fancy horses, and when we made the eighteen-mile journey in three hours to visit Grandmother, it was speed to talk about, quite as exciting as a jet plane ride today. And Grandma added another skill to the skills of my mother. She took the wheat straws and made beautiful braid, which she sewed into hats for all the family.

As you know, there were no movies, TV, or radio or any commercial entertainment; but locally produced theatricals were most exciting. You knew the hero and villain personally, which added to the interest. Everyone who wished to, had an opportunity to take part in the entertainment productions. Between acts there were songs, recitations, and instrumental musical selections. The weekly dances were a community activity, where young and old danced the quadrille, the schottische, and the Virginia reel together. What fun!

There were no hospitals, doctors, or registered nurses, so the health of the community was everyone's concern. The Relief Society sisters were real angels of mercy, caring for the sick and comforting the distressed. When there was a death, it was the Relief Society sisters who cared for the body, made the burial clothes, and dressed the corpse. The men made the coffin, and the sisters lined it carefully. The grave was dug by friends, and when the coffin was lowered, the friends carefully covered the grave, while everyone stayed to comfort the mourners. The sorrow of one was the sorrow of the entire community.

I am grateful for the wonderful modern conveniences and for all the exciting developments modern science has brought us. But I know they do not automatically bring happiness. There were some advantages in the busy, self-sufficient days of yesteryear. Some of that simple life can be recaptured with family camping trips or visits to rural areas. Such experiences should help us to reevaluate and remind us that we should not take our luxuries for granted nor consider them all-important. Happiness is achieved in individuals, not by flights to the moon or Mars, but in the satisfaction of mature adjustment to life as we find it.

5

Christmas Memories

Manuscript 1985 (Edited version in
This People Magazine, Dec. 1985/Jan. 1986)

I was born in the Mormon colony called Colonia Juarez
in northern Mexico in 1894. We lived in a little brick cottage
that backed on the Piedras Verdes River. My father's mother
lived a short distance upriver, and after I was big enough I
was sent every day to carry milk to her in a small tin bucket
with a wire bail. The bucket was so heavy that the wire
handle cut into the little finger of my right hand and caused
a permanent scar there.

One Christmas morning, when I was about ten, we had
opened our presents and I was sent on my daily errand. As
I walked along I saw, to my horror, smoke and flames shooting
from the fine two-story brick home of the Stowells, through
the block. Adelia Stowell, my age, was a special friend. In a
panic I ran home, crying to my parents, "Oh, the Stowells'
house is on fire. Their Christmas will be gone!" The candles
on their Christmas tree had tipped and started a blaze that

47

quickly engulfed the whole house. They had time to save almost nothing. But in that close-knit community the neighbors came forward to fill their needs and to share Christmas with them. I secretly envied Adelia a little, because she ended up having more for Christmas than ever, because of the fire. I know the family would have been helped, whatever the time of year, but the outpouring of generosity seemed especially appropriate for Christmas Day, when traditionally we enjoy a special readiness to share.

In Mexico we made our own decorations. We could not afford glass baubles and tinsel then, but Christmas was no less fun for that. We popped corn and used a needle to string the puffed white kernels on thread. We looped these long white strings on the tree, along with the paper chains we made of varicolored construction paper. At one time we used lighted candles on the tree too, but the Stowells' terrifying experience persuaded us to abandon that.

When I went to school the children tried to tell me there was no Santa Claus, that he was just your parents. I was horrified at the suggestion. It couldn't be. I refused to believe it. Santa could bring me anything my heart desired. He might choose not to, but he could do it, and that allowed my fantasy full rein. My friends pitied me, yet I knew what I knew. Then on Christmas Eve I went to bed but lay awake, excited at the prospect of wonderful things on Christmas morning. Finally I heard the sound of a toy wagon being trundled into the living room and heard the toot of a toy horn—and my father's laugh. "It is Papa! It is!" I cried in despair. All my hopes of fantastic gifts evaporated.

After I married Spencer Kimball, we created our own pattern for observing Christmas. For example, because there were morning chores to be done, we always expected that milking the cows and other responsibilties be taken care of first. Perhaps because I was a home economics teacher concerned about nutrition, I insisted that everyone had to finish breakfast. Finally we sat around the Christmas tree in the living room while Spencer handed out the gifts one by one, so that everyone could watch and enjoy the opening of others' presents. It is not that this is "the right way," just that it is "our way."

I recall one Christmas Eve out of the ordinary. In 1961 my husband, Spencer, and I and the Howard W. Hunters made a long pilgrimage to Bethlehem to experience Advent. We expected to enjoy a special sense of what Christmas meant by being there where it had all happened. We envisioned Bethlehem as a quiet little village, but we found instead that on Christmas Eve people had gathered there from all over the world. Instead of peace, we found crowds milling around and a sound truck in the town square blaring out Christmas carols. We could hardly move. We negotiated with difficulty the steps down into the crypt of the Church of the Nativity, to the traditional site of the long-ago stable. The noise and crowding oppressed us, and we soon made our way out to the open air again, somewhat disappointed.

Then we found our way to the field where tradition says the shepherds had been watching their flocks by night when Christ was born. We stood there alone in the quiet countryside. The moon beamed brightly and the stars shown so brilliantly that one could imagine how it might have been when that special star moved in the sky and the angels brought glad tidings. We looked toward the town two miles away and sang, just the few of us, "O Little Town of Bethlehem" and "Far, Far Away on Judea's Plains." We prayed in gratitude and gloried in the feelings of the moment. It is impossible to recapture in words our emotions, but each Christmas I have tried.

In our family on Christmas Eve we have ordinarily included reading about the birth of Christ from the scriptures. As we have acquired grandchildren, Christmas Eve has become a time to act the story out, complete with shepherds, angels, and wise men in makeshift costumes. The grandfather and fathers have taken the role of camels and donkeys. There is always a girl to be Mary and usually a baby to portray the Christ-child. The little children always look forward to the reenactment, as I read the familiar words from St. Luke.

In common with most families, we always have a Christmas tree. One year, a few weeks before Christmas, I thought out loud, "We're getting older; I think I'll not bother with a tree this year." A fifteen-year-old granddaughter heard me and exclaimed, aghast at the thought, "Oh, Grandma!" That was enough to change my mind. We bought and decorated a Christmas tree, as we always had.

In my neighborhood five young women lived together in a house. As my visiting teaching companion and I called on them one Saturday in December, we found them sitting on the floor making Christmas decorations. They were participating in the "Sub for Santa" program, providing Christmas for a woman with four small children who had been deserted by her husband. They had learned about the family's needs and were busily gathering food and clothing and toys to share, without expecting anything in return.

Another neighbor, an elderly widow, showed me a small basket of homemade cookies she had found on her doorstep with a note: "Merry Christmas from your 'Secret Granddaughter'!"

Friends once gave my husband fifty dollars as "a birthday gift for the Savior" and asked him to find someone who had a special need for the money. That gift made it possible for two worthy women in Europe who would not otherwise have been able to have that blessing to attend the dedication of the temple in Switzerland. Spencer explained to the friends what he had done with their gift. They were pleased and the next year gave one hundred dollars. That money brought a dying man and his family from Mexico to be sealed in the temple before his death. And each year for many years after that our friends took pleasure in giving money anonymously.

Christmas is a time of many traditions. In this culture we give gifts to family and friends, we decorate our homes with Christmas symbols, we sing songs and tell stories that remind us of the birth of Christ, and we greet even strangers with a warmer smile.

Traditions are not inherently good; some are bad or dangerous, such as using real candles on the Christmas tree. We have known generally sober people who considered it part of the Christmas season to get drunk. And we know of holiday office parties where appropriate restraints are let down, as though what was done on this one occasion did not really count. But good traditions, which embody truth and righteous doing, reinforce our good intentions. Traditions also provide a link to the past, tying us to those whose traditions we follow. It is valuable, therefore, for families to build good traditions.

It is actually less important what the traditions are than that we establish some pattern. The continuity contributes to a sense of security. There may be traditional foods, such as oyster stew for Christmas Eve or an orange in the stocking or turkey for holiday dinner. Perhaps the same worn tree-top ornament crowns the tree each year, whatever other decorations may change. One of our sons has incorporated Christmas customs from the country where he served his mission; this gives a special flavor to the holiday and at the same time reminds the children of their missionary heritage. Or father may get the same gift under the tree year after year — in one case I know, a waddling mechanical elephant, brought out year after year.

We often worry too much about what to give. We say, of a neighbor or friend or relative, "They always give us such a nice gift. What could we give that would be adequate? They have everything." The giving of presents is a good tradition, reinforcing the impulse to generosity, though it sometimes degenerates to an empty exchange. It can greatly reduce the strain if we establish the tradition of giving small gifts, thoughtfully made or chosen. Market value is not important; care in selection is. Gifts we have made, with love, count for more.

We have enjoyed receiving letters and home-made Christmas cards from our family members. From the little grandchildren and great-grandchildren come folded papers with drawings and laboriously printed with "I love you" and "Merry Christmas." A thoughtful letter from a loved one far outweighs, in my scales, a gift from the store.

Nothing we can buy will last forever, but love will, and character. By giving love and helping our families develop the Christ-like trait of unselfishness, we can lay the foundation for eternities of joy with our family and with all those who inherit the celestial kingdom.

Christmas is a good time for developing generosity; it is so much easier then, when the world seems filled with good will. But ultimately our objective is to follow our King in loving all people at all times, looking for the opportunity to give help—a letter to a lonely person, a kind word, a smile, a charitable gift—as the need arises, without waiting for a calendared occasion.

I pray continually that we will build traditions of giving the "good gifts" in the assurance that God has given us the greatest of all gifts, the opportunity for eternal life through Jesus Christ.

6

Visiting Teaching

Ensign Stake, May 6, 1976

I salute you, my dear sisters, for having accepted a choice opportunity to show your love for Christ by accepting one of the most practical and effective ways of demonstrating your love for him: by your concern for others.

When asked by one of the Pharisees, "Master, which is the great commandment," Jesus answered, "Thou shalt love the Lord thy God with all thy heart, and with all thy soul, and with all thy mind. This is the first and great commandment. And the second is like unto it, Thou shalt love thy neighbour as thyself. On these two commandments hang all the law and the prophets." (Matthew 22:36-40.)

To those who professed love for him, the Lord said, "If ye love me, keep my commandments. . . . He that hath my commandments, and keepeth them, he it is that loveth me." (John 14:15, 21.)

A philosopher put it in these words: "The first fundamental truth about our individual lives is the indispensability of love to every human being. By love I mean relatedness to some treasured person or group, the feeling of being of value to others. Our interdependence with others is the most all-encompassing fact of human reality; our personalities are made up by our contacts with others."

In answer to the question "Who is my neighbour?" Jesus told the parable of the Good Samaritan. Thus did he teach one of the most important principles of the gospel — mercy and love, a principle we must learn to live if we truly would be his disciples and help bring lasting peace to the earth.

Even though we may never have the opportunity to help an injured stranger along the roadside, in our assignment as visiting teachers we have responsibility to a group of our sisters, any one of whom may have a special need for our assistance. Sometimes we leave tasks for others that are our specified responsibility. I feel fortunate to have had fifty years of this opportunity, and I plan to continue as long as I may be called to this service.

I think of the priesthood home teachers and the Relief Society visiting teachers as constituting a great umbrella of protection over all the members of the Church, worldwide. Every Latter-day Saint has at least two personal contacts with authorized teachers and friends at least once a month, with the privilege of an eye-to-eye and heart-to-heart visit. It is a reciprocal service. I guard and care for you, and someone is equally concerned for my welfare.

President J. Reuben Clark said many times about church service, "It doesn't matter where you serve, but only how." It is well for us to look at our record occasionally to see if there is room for improvement. When we visit an inactive member, we may be the only personal contact with the Church that she has. In some such cases I have succeeded in helping activate the member, but in other cases I have failed. I am still concerned for them.

As we visit, we should be sensitive to any need, and not just physical want. There may be bitterness, feelings of neglect, sickness, loneliness, or despondency. In times of sorrow we should be the first on hand to offer help. "A friend in need is a friend indeed."

We should prepare for visits. The ward preparation meeting helps through discussions of the lessons we are to carry. If we visit early in the month, there will be time for repeat visits as needed. A regular time allows your sisters to expect you. You and your companion should pray together, on your knees if practical. You should discuss how to present the lesson to each person. Not all can be approached the same way. Go with a spirit of love, not criticism. The lesson is best as a discussion rather than a lecture. Without prying, be sensitive to the special needs you may find. Maintain confidentiality about any problems, except as the Relief Society president may need to know. Do your utmost to make the visit pleasant, so you leave with an assurance that you will be welcome when you come again.

Your visit is only part of your responsibility. Make a point to speak to the sisters in your district as you see them at church, at Relief Society, in town, or anyplace you may meet. To *have* a friend, you must *be* one. Just last week I met an inactive sister whom I used to visit. She seemed glad to see me. I urged her again to come to Relief Society. She said she knows she should and that she would try.

The friends I have made through visiting teaching and their expressions of appreciation provide some of the rewards for my efforts. But I know that we must be prepared also for failures. One sister in our district never let us into her home. Though we were often sure she was home, she did not answer the door. I sent her a card when her neighbor told me she was sick. One day we happened along just as she was taking in her garbage cans from the street. She could hardly refuse to see us, but even then her reception was cold. I wondered what the trouble could be. I asked her neighbor, and she told me that some years ago the woman had had sickness and trouble in her home and felt that the

Church had neglected her and her family, so they had turned their back on the Church and all its functions. There are too many such sad cases, sometimes caused by our neglect.

Another sister had been inaccessible to us. Early in January I called and told her that her Relief Society teachers would like to call at her home and wish her a happy New Year. She said, "Well, can't you do it on the phone?" "We will take just a minute of your time, if we may call," I explained. "All right," she said. When she came to the door, she had a big Saint Bernard dog by her side and did not invite us in. Our only satisfaction was that we had wished her a happy New Year and had seen her face to face for the first time.

But in all my years, these are the only complete failures I can remember. There have been successes. One woman who was inactive began to come to me with her problems and has subsequently become very active in Relief Society. Another sister, a widow, moved out of our ward and into a rest home, and I used to continue to visit her there for several years, until she died. We always left an elderly couple for last, because they urged us to stay as long as we could. When the woman died, her husband was so lonely that I continued to visit him until he, too, died.

In city wards where members live close to one another, travel is little problem, but some of our sisters make great sacrifices. Some years ago our daughter-in-law living in Michigan traveled sixty miles round trip to visit one of the sisters. "But she is so thrilled to see us, since she rarely has a chance to go to church, that it is worth the effort," she told me.

A Relief Society president in Chile assigned herself to visit a sister who lived on a mountain. To get to the woman's house, this visiting teacher hiked for over an hour on a steep, dry, rocky path. Another pair of visiting teachers reported visiting a sister who would not receive them. She always had excuses about how busy she was, and had no time to listen to their message. But the teachers continued to visit, though they found the rejection unpleasant. Finally the woman began coming to Relief Society; later she accepted a position of responsibility in the ward, and thereafter she continued actively involved in the Church.

A blueprint for our guidance is 2 Nephi 31:20: "Wherefore, ye must press forward with a steadfastness in Christ, having a perfect brightness of hope, and a love of God and of all men. Wherefore, if ye press forward, feasting upon the word of Christ, and endure to the end, behold, thus saith the Father: Ye shall have eternal life" — the greatest gift of God to man. I can suggest no more sure way to place ourselves on this path than to be the most faithful and effective visiting teachers we are capable of being.

7

A Woman's Preparation

Paris Area Conference, July 31, 1976

My dear brothers and sisters, I appreciate this special opportunity to speak especially to the mothers and daughters at this conference. This is a precious relationship and an opportunity for developing greater love and understanding between mothers and daughters. I treasure the memory of my own mother and think often of what she means to me. I look forward with great anticipation to seeing her again someday. We have only one daughter, and I'm so very grateful for her precious companionship.

As members of The Church of Jesus Christ of Latter-day Saints, we all have common ideals and objectives. The Church is a universal brotherhood and sisterhood. We know the importance of the family and are grateful for the comprehensive programs designed for our Monday evening family gatherings. I am sure we think of this as a sacred gospel direction and follow it as faithfully as all other teachings designed for our happiness and best good.

We of the Church have the knowledge that the family may be the eternal unit of importance if the marriage is sealed for eternity in the holy temple of God. The role of the successful mother is a lifetime of dedication. It is the most exacting and difficult of all professions. Anyone who would say apologetically, "I am only a homemaker," has not fully appreciated the importance and intricacy of her profession. Some of the attributes required to be successful are an unlimited amount of love and patience, unselfishness, and endurance.

A woman should be skilled in child training, in psychology and sociology, in economics and management, in nutrition and nursing. In fact, a well-rounded education will be a great help in caring for and training a family.

There should be love and harmony between husband and wife. In the home is the opportunity for the mother to teach her children to honor and respect their father, who holds the priesthood of God. It is he who will properly preside and direct the activities of the family.

Children should be cherished with the strongest bonds of affection. No sacrifice is too great to protect our family from evil and to rear them in righteousness. Our constant anxiety is that all family members will live worthy of the eternal blessings promised to those who remain faithful to the end. The sanctity of the home must be zealously guarded, for it is here that the morality and righteous habits are formed.

Children have an equal responsibility to contribute to the security. There must be complete confidence and trust between parents and children. Obedience of children to parents is essential to peace in the home. Unselfishness on the part of each member of the family is basic to happiness there.

First and foremost, a woman must learn to do intelligent mothering. This is more than highly emotionalized mothering which showers love and affection upon the child and which might lead her to uphold him in wrongdoing. She must realize that the child's future, to a large extent, is measured in the mother's ability to influence and direct him wisely. In the home must be taught faith, self-control, honesty, and loyalty. The gospel of work must be a part of the child's training. There must be provided the environment for the development of the child physically, morally, emotionally, and spiritually. We should constantly hold up the child to his very best efforts.

The genuine mother takes time to reach out beyond her own children and sense her responsibility to help all children. Wherever a child is found cold, hungry, or in need of attention or care of any kind, a good mother will render loving and intelligent service. In the home in which there is an intelligent and spiritually strong mother dwells the greatest single influence on the spiritual and moral strength of the family nurtured there.

I would hope that every girl and woman here has the desire and ambition to qualify in two vocations — that of homemaking, and that of preparing to earn a living outside the home, if and when the occasion requires. An unmarried woman is always happier if she has a vocation in which she can be socially of service and financially independent. In no case should she be urged to accept an unworthy companion as a means of support. Any married woman may become a widow without warning. Property may vanish as readily as a husband may die. Thus, any woman may be under the necessity of earning her own living and helping to support dependent children. If she has been trained for the duties and the emergencies of life which may come to her, she will be much happier and have a greater sense of security.

Another valid reason for a woman to prepare herself to fulfill a vocation is that not all of her lifetime could possibly be completely filled with demands of a family, home, and children. The later years of a woman's life should be viewed as a time that can be socially and professionally productive.

When a mother's children are reared, or if she is childless, the years after forty or fifty may begin to look bleak. Her real life's work may seem done, when in reality it has only changed. The active woman cannot hold her hands, so she looks about for something to take up her leisure time. What should it be? Charity? General meddlesomeness? Shall she become a burden or shall she embark upon a new adventure?

Happy the woman who has the foresight to see that through forty years of experience, she has matured the ability to commence a grand and useful second half of her life. Let her study a profession or adopt a trade, or find some absorbing subject for study and research. There are many learning opportunities for senior citizens. This is a rare opportunity for advanced study in some subject of special interest. There is no place nor time when one can justify idly sitting by to vegetate. Keeping mentally, physically, and spiritually growing constantly is the way to continue the happy, useful life.

The Church holds special challenges in temple and missionary work. Genealogical research is also challenging and calls for workers. If one has a literary talent, active or latent, these are choice years to be productive in this area. Have you written your own autobiography or the biography of a father, mother, or grandparent who did not get this important work done? We all owe it to ourselves, our posterity, and our relatives to leave a written record of our life's activities.

In addition, there are many opportunities for service to others. The world is full of lonely, troubled people who need a helping hand, who need a listening ear or a friendly visit or a comforting letter. Our watchword should be "Never stop growing and serving."

We have talked about the importance of good family relations, about the importance of a woman's education, and about intelligent mothering, of giving of ourselves to others in service. And some may ask, "Where can I get help in achieving all of these objectives?" Sisters, we women of the

Church of Jesus Christ are most fortunate to have an organization revealed to a prophet of God that is designed to help us in achieving and fulfilling all of our basic needs. We have the Relief Society organization specifically for this very purpose. If there are any of you eligible for membership in this organization who have not taken advantage of it, I would urge you to do so. Its varied programs are designed for our growth and happiness. There is opportunity for participation for each member. It's a wonderful place to make friends and be of service. I would urge you to be active in this great worldwide sisterhood of the Church now. The visiting teaching program is designed to give us the opportunity to have and be a friend in need. I should like to tell you that it has been my privilege to serve for more than fifty years as a visiting teacher in the wards in which I have lived, and I find great joy and satisfaction in this opportunity.

I bear my testimony to the truthfulness of the gospel of Jesus Christ and express my deep gratitude to my Heavenly Father for membership in his church and kingdom. I know that Christ is our Redeemer, and I express my love for him. And I pray for each of us, that we may know the joy and satisfaction of membership and service in his church.

8

We Will Give the Tenth unto Thee

Relief Society Magazine, April 1945

"The earth is the Lord's, and the fulness thereof" (Psalm 24:1), and we, his children, are only stewards of his domain. It is given to us to enjoy the fullness of the bounty of the earth, and in return it is required that we pay one tenth of our increase for the building up of the kingdom of God and for the furtherance of his work on the earth.

The laws of the gospel of Jesus Christ are made plain to us, his children. The "abundant life," spoken of so often by Christ, is the joyous life that comes from sacrifice, struggle, and accomplishment. Some may feel that the law of tithing is difficult, but if it is, the blessings that come from its observance, in added strength of character and power to overcome temptation, bring us proportionately nearer the "abundant life."

The law of tithing comes down to us from earliest biblical history. Cain did not bring an honest tithing before the Lord, while Abel did. Abraham and Jacob paid tithes. The law was repeated to Moses on Mount Sinai. By modern revelation the law was first given as the standing law of the Church on July 8, 1838. Under the inspired leadership of Lorenzo Snow, the Church members were stimulated to more fully obey the law, and by their so doing, financial security and the means to build temples and spread the gospel in many countries of the world has been made possible. However, the work yet to be done is vast beyond our comprehension, and we should be fired by new enthusiasm to live this law more fully.

Church statistics show that the greatest amount of tithing is paid in December, an exemplification of the human weakness of procrastination. The proper time to pay our tithing is at the time our income is received, be that weekly, monthly, by season, or annually. Those who leave it to the last of the year find a multitude of expenses facing them, which makes it increasingly hard to be honest with the Lord. Even the best of intentions may then be thwarted, and thus we deprive ourselves of the blessings that come to the tithe payer.

The glow of satisfaction does not come to the one who has been niggardly with his offerings. It is amusing, and yet a bit pathetic, to listen to a discussion of what is an honest tithing sometimes heard in a Sunday School class. Some suggest all possible deductions that might be made, seeming to be more anxious to pay as little as will salve their consciences, rather than recognizing the opportunity to receive the blessings which come from a knowledge of having lived the law without reservation. In Moroni 7:6 we read, "For behold, God hath said a man being evil cannot do that which is good; for if he offereth a gift, or prayeth unto God, except he shall do it with real intent it profiteth him nothing." The blessing comes through the intent of the heart. Only our Heavenly Father and we ourselves know whether we give wholeheartedly with a feeling of gratitude and thanksgiving or with a feeling of compulsion or parsimony.

There are those Church members who worry about the use to which the Church funds are put. It is interesting to notice that it is not the full tithe payer who is thus concerned, but usually the member who wishes to find an excuse for his nonpayment of tithes in declaration of his disapproval of the handling of the funds. One wealthy member of the Church, living in a small community, openly declared that he would not pay tithing, but that each year he would give a sizable sum to some public charity or needy individual, for which he received newspaper publicity. He was heard to say, "I think I am a better judge of where my money will do the most good than the bishop or Church authorities are." This man gave to be seen of men and so has his reward. The tithe payer who gives with love and trust, unlauded by men, surely will receive a far greater reward, for he is storing up for himself treasures in heaven.

In obeying the law of tithing, we have a tangible way of showing that our religion is not merely a form, but a living, active force in our everyday lives. In times of stress, such as the period in which we are now living, we feel, more than at any other time, a real need for activity to combat the evils at work around us. We cannot give passive lip service and keep our faith live. What more definite, combative force can be found than the act of going all the way in the payment of an honest tithing to our Heavenly Father?

Our boys who are fighting on the battle fronts all over the world are fortifying themselves with the force of true, honest living by sending their tithing from India, Alaska, Africa, Italy, England, and the islands of the Pacific. Their letters bear testimony of the strength this tangible act of obedience gives them. It is a strand in the lifeline that ties them closely to the body of the Church and to our Heavenly Father. This is no lip service, but a concrete evidence of a desire to obey the commandments and so be worthy of blessings.

As Latter-day Saint parents, our responsibility to our children is not complete when we provide them with food, shelter, and clothing. We are commanded: "They shall also teach their children to pray, and to walk uprightly before the Lord." (D&C 68:28.) There is a definite time to teach a child to pay tithing, and it should not be postponed until he is old enough to earn an income outside the home. An opportunity should be made for children, when they are very young, to earn their spending money by doing, regularly and well, definite chores at home. They should then be taught to budget their money carefully, and that the first tenth belongs to the Lord and is not theirs to spend otherwise. Thus, they will learn the habits of honesty, thrift, and independence. The payment of tithing can easily be made a habit if there is never an exception allowed, even though children may feel they need the money for something else.

Sometimes children earn money and carefully save it for a special purpose, but are tempted to let the Lord wait until later for that which is his. Parents would do well to be firm in permitting no exception to the rule that the tithe comes first; it is not ours to spend. It should be designated for the one, sacred purpose. Thousands will testify to the greater joy and strength that come from strict and unfaltering obedience to this law of the gospel.

In preparing a Young Women's Mutual Improvement Association class of young girls for an excursion to the temple to be baptized for the dead, I was astonished to find how many of them had never paid tithing or felt they had ever owed any. Many of them earned small allowances at home, but they just had not been taught that this should be tithed. We learn to do only by doing, and it is most important that parents create the opportunity for very young children to form this habit. Some parents make the excuse that it would be a burden for the bishop to put a child's name on the tithing record for a very small sum. Any bishop worthy of the calling feels a real thrill when a child comes to pay his tithing, even it if be only a dime. A child's tithing receipts should be among his most prized possessions, tangible evidence of his worthy standing in the Church—not to be exhibited, but for his own satisfaction. The amount is not the important thing; the child's or the widow's small tenth is just as acceptable in the eyes of the Lord as the thousands paid by the rich man.

The Lord has spoken through his prophet Malachi: "Bring ye all the tithes into the storehouse, that there may be meat in mine house, and prove me now herewith, saith the Lord of hosts, if I will not open you the windows of heaven, and pour you out a blessing, that there shall not be room enough to receive it." (Malachi 3:10.) Blessings of health and of harmony in the home, the feelings of peace and well-being in one's soul and of love and good will toward one's neighbors, cannot be bought with money, but only by keeping the commandments. These blessings may be ours if we can say, as did Jacob, "And of all that thou shalt give me I will surely give the tenth unto thee." (Genesis 28:22.)

9

Mother: Call Her Blessed

Mother's Day, 1978

"Her children arise up, and call her blessed; her husband also, and he praiseth her." (Proverbs 31:28.)

Sometimes you may hear a woman say, as if apologetically, "I'm only a mother." Many don't express it this way but seem to act as if they believed it. They are selling themselves short indeed, for true motherhood is the greatest calling a woman can have. "A woman who rears successfully a family of healthy, worthy sons and daughters," said President David O. McKay, "whose influence will be felt through generations to come, is living for eternity. She deserves the highest honor that man can give and the choicest blessings of God."

We frequently hear the expression, "Mothers are partners with God." Hear this as it flashes by you in a talk in church and you may miss its impact. Ponder it in an hour of private meditation in your own home and you will marvel anew at its import. The earthly mothers of God's spirit children! The mortal mentors of those who for eons have dwelt in God's presence and been instructed under his direction! What a glorious and privileged opportunity!

Think for a moment of Mary, the mother of Jesus. Recall the visit of the angel announcing the forthcoming birth — the wonder and the joy of it, the literal Son of God to be given an earthly tabernacle through her! None of us, of course, would seek to equate our calling with that of Mary or to compare our own children with the divine Savior. But the parallels are unquestionably there. We too are partners with God in furthering his plan. We too are partners with God in providing earthly tabernacles for his spirit children. We too are essential links in the chain of earthly experience which since the time of Adam and Eve has been providing the mortal testing-ground that is the gateway to immortality and eternal life.

And especially when we consider the latter-day mother in Israel, the channel to mortality for the spirits held in reserve for the culminating period in the earth's history as the millennial reign approaches, does anybody who has a true understanding dare to call her "only a mother"? Rather, let us choose the words of Proverbs. Let us call her "blessed."

It was Adam and Eve who first received and obeyed the Lord's commandment to "multiply and replenish the earth" and who thereby established upon this earth the divine institution of the family. To us today the commandment is just as forthright, and compliance brings to us also the same mixed package of joy and sadness, fulfillment and frustration, as Adam and Eve must have experienced. The institution our first parents began has been the basis of society ever since.

Increasingly, perceptive authors are linking the success of our civilization to the importance of the family, noting that throughout history nations have been able to survive many types of disasters, including invasions, earthquakes, famines, and depressions, whereas the disintegration of the family has spelled their doom. As a church and a people we understand why this is so. The family is an eternal unit in God's plan—the eternal unit, it would be correct to say—since nothing supersedes that unit in importance, or outlasts it. Small wonder, then, that earthly kingdoms, empires, and republics, needing all they can get of wisdom and strength, fall apart when they discard the stability represented by the God-ordained organization of the family.

And if the family is the basis of society, what is the basis of the family? There might be more than one answer to this question, but high on the list must come the role of mother. The commandment to teach our children gospel principles, for example, is given to parents—and not just to one of them, though in practice it often tends to become a delegated authority. The father's role takes him away on legitimate family concerns. The mother is there on the spot—or normally should be. On whom, then, does the day-to-day rearing of the children in their early years naturally fall? Abraham Lincoln was not the only one who owed all that he was or ever hoped to be to his mother. Myriads of less expressive souls who are unknown to fame are similarly indebted to mother.

It is this crucial, key role in the basic unit of society that is under attack today. The great propaganda machines are spilling their dangerous nonsense that it is in some way demeaning for a woman to be "merely" a wife, mother, and homemaker, and that her self-respect and her equal status demand that she pursue a career in law, medicine, or business. Those who advocate this simply do not understand the true priorities, the eternal priorities. We are not here on earth primarily to make money, or to achieve worldly acclaim, or to carve out a career that at best ends at death. The associates of the woman immersed in a career of law, medicine, or business may call her by such terms as doctor, professor, or president, but for the woman who has the opportunity to marry well and raise children to the Lord, such titles are no substitutes for the real thing. The real thing gives her a simpler and a more enduring title: blessed. "Her children shall arise up, and call her blessed," says the scripture, and to me that means the two-syllable kind of blessed. Who can doubt that the woman who successfully fulfills her God-ordained career will one day receive that same tribute from the Lord himself?

Most of the problems of child waywardness and adolescent upheaval are related to a lack of parental discipline and influence in the home. Obviously the risks are greater when the mother chooses to pursue a career outside the home. When a working mother comes home from a day at the factory, office, or school and takes up her responsibilities as homemaker, she is already tired. Generally she cannot devote to her children, or even to her husband, the attention they need; and when they feel neglected or unimportant, it will not be long before cracks begin to appear in the fabric of the family life.

This is not to suggest that there are not sometimes circumstances, even when the children are young, that require a mother to go to work. What I am suggesting is that, for the LDS mother with children at home, that decision should be made only for compelling reasons and after receiving guidance of the Spirit to that effect. My appeal is that we make such a decision in the wisdom of eternal ideals and concepts rather than rationalizing away a birthright that permits us to bear and rear in mortality and take with us into the eternities the spirit children of our Father who have been assigned to our care.

When I think of a mother raising her children, my mind goes back to my own wonderful mother. I grew up in a small Mormon community in Old Mexico. My father was a cattle rancher and farmer. Both he and my mother were of pioneer parentage and had suffered the privations of frontier life. We were trained in strict economy. "Waste not, want not" was the watchword of our home.

Mother had a way of making each of her eight living children feel special. She showered us with love and adoration, but at the same time she was a strict disciplinarian. We were taught to work as soon as we were able to do even the smallest of tasks. I remember that as a very young child I was assigned the job of dusting the intricate iron grillwork on the frame of the sewing machine. It seemed an endless task, but when I finished it, the praise given by my mother was ample pay.

As children we were each impressed with the importance of always doing our very best, of excelling. We were urged to take every opportunity to fill special assignments — to give a talk, learn a poem, or sing a song. Mother always followed up our preparation and participation with smiling commendation when we did well.

My mother was an avid reader herself and encouraged us to read good books. She was an optimist. The world was beautiful in her eyes, and people were good. She would not allow unkind criticism of anyone, especially criticism of the bishop or anyone in authority.

Mother was independent and scrupulously honest. If we earned a dollar, we were reminded of the tenth part that belonged to the Lord for tithing.

I never knew her to be late for a meeting or for any appointment. In fact, she was always there ahead of time. She was completely unselfish, always concerned for the welfare and pleasure of others. She visited the poor and the sick and always carried food, flowers, or magazines to those she visited. Her Church service was continuous all of her life. For many years she was the much-loved president of the YWMIA, and then of the Relief Society. She was always a teacher in one or more of the organizations.

To be a successful wife and mother (and, I might add, grandmother) is the greatest challenge a woman can face. Her job qualifications include patience, love unbounded, understanding, unselfishness, endurance, fidelity, and spiritual guidance. Her vocational responsibilities include those of dietician, cook, housecleaner, laundress, interior decorator, accountant, nurse, and many others. Not only must she be proficient in household arts, but she needs to understand psychology, sociology, and psychiatry as well. She must be skilled in child rearing, in communication, in management. Motherhood is indeed a highly responsible career. In addition, a wife needs to keep her husband happy and to improve her mental and spiritual powers so as to assure her own happiness and development.

And when the children are all reared, happy is the mother who is prepared to cheerfully redirect her energies to useful pursuits and interests that will challenge her for the rest of her life. Some of these may be joint interests with her husband, interests that time now permits her to pursue. Some certainly should be in the line of service, for, as King Benjamin said, "when ye are in the service of your fellow beings ye are only in the service of your God." (Mosiah 2:17.)

That thought brings us full circle, back to the mother's greatest service of all, her service to those "fellow beings" closest to her— her family. By that service she is privileged to train potential bishops, stake presidents, Relief Society and Primary presidents, or other leaders and teachers in our Father's kingdom. Looking beyond mortality's brief span, she is training souls for godhood. When that service is well done, will not those sons and daughters in maturity "arise up, and call her blessed"? And will she not be among those "on the right hand" of whom on judgment day the King shall say, "Come, ye blessed of my Father"?

Yes, whatever other titles and names Mother may be known by, that one is paramount. That is the role which, if she fulfills it conscientiously, is the most likely to earn her the eternal rewards we all seek.

10

Let Every Day Be Mother's Day

Relief Society Magazine, May 1948

The observance of Mother's Day has become an impressive outward demonstration of latent love and gratitude to mothers. It comes by a gift, words of appreciation, acts of kindness, or letters on the part of everyone. Mother is a magic word, calling forth a train of memories in the mind of each individual, accompanied by a variety of emotions depending upon how some woman has fulfilled this sacred trust.

Motherhood is a career of the first magnitude and is the instinctive ambition of every girl. Nature may endow her with the physical potentiality of motherhood, but to become an ideal mother will take the combined training of home, church, and school. Above all must come her own realization of the tremendous responsibility this sacred calling entails.

Her physical, mental, moral, emotional, and spiritual development are of prime importance to the generation she mothers.

To be daughter, mother, and grandmother is to make the destined cycle of womanhood and to know the joys, responsibilities, and development these experiences bring. Because they call for personal sacrifice and self-mastery, their value is enhanced. The child accepts the care and devotion of a self-sacrificing mother as a birthright. But the law of life exacts full payment for everything we get. This nurturing of our children may be repaid in part by loving devotion to parents, but the debt is never paid in full until the child becomes the parent and so in turn cares for a succeeding generation. The laws of God operate in perfect justice and bring happiness so long as we live in accordance with them. It is only when we selfishly seek to thwart them that troubles and disappointments come. The laws of compensation and retribution are never failing, though payment may sometimes be deferred. There may amass an ever larger and larger debt, but eventually it must be liquidated. Wise indeed is the individual who pays as he goes in so far as this is possible. Love, and you shall be loved. Serve, and you shall receive service.

Protective mother love is the guardian of youth, but protection too long continued makes for weakness, not strength, in the child. To watch the tiny, helpless infant grow and develop under your constant, watchful care is to see a miracle wrought. To live again in the enthusiasm and activity of youth with your children is to intensify and enrich life's drama. To be counselor and protector, knowing when to assist and when to recede into the background, that your child may learn to walk alone, calls for almost superhuman wisdom. Wise indeed is the mother who has found the source of divine aid through prayer and who begins with the little child at her knee, teaching that child to pray to our all-wise Heavenly Father for the strength that will protect him or her against the forces of evil. A true mother's objective is to teach and train wisely until she can say with assurance, "My children are strong enough to walk alone with faith as their guide."

That home is ideal where the true, spiritual perspective of life is the operating force. Not what is expedient or what will bring immediate satisfaction will be the governing factors, but what are lasting and eternal values. The mother can do much to establish the spiritual tone of the home. She must first have deep-grounded faith herself. She must be emotionally stabilized and self-controlled so that her own feelings may not interfere with the frictionless operation of her home. It will be she who arranges schedules so that there may be time for regular, peaceful family devotion. She must be persistent in planning and helping carry forward the family evenings, family picnics, and other occasions that will build family solidarity and common interests. One of the greatest safeguards children can have is the knowledge that their mother trusts them and that the family looks to them to maintain family standards and family honor.

"It is more blessed to give than to receive" is an axiom often misapplied by some mothers. In their anxiety to serve their children, they forget that there must be reciprocity in giving if all are to share in the blessings. If they insist on doing all the giving, they deprive their children of the joy of service. Some mothers enjoy being martyrs. They get a certain morbid satisfaction out of feeling that they do all the giving and take nothing in return. Mothers must learn to accept favors graciously and appreciatively so that children may know this satisfaction. Often it is easier to do a job than to accept the untrained help of children, but they can learn to do only by doing.

At the other extreme are the spoiled, pampered mothers who feel that they have brought children into the world at great personal sacrifice and are justified in exacting unmeasured servitude in return. They continually complain of aches and pains. They are habitually tired, nervous, and irritable. They enjoy being waited upon and continually remind the children of the great debt owed to mother.

Between these two extremes is the well-adjusted mother who accepts motherhood as the greatest blessing and the greatest opportunity life can offer. She takes good care of her own health so that she may more efficiently care for her family. She is careful of her personal appearance so that her family may be proud of her, realizing that there may be times when it will be wiser to buy a new dress for herself than something extra for the children. She knows that an immaculate house may not always be a happy home. She keeps up constructive interests outside her home so that she may be a more vital and interesting individual. She remembers that she must be a good wife as well as a good mother, striving to keep abreast of her husband so that when the children leave the home nest, they too may still find true companionship in life's evening.

Full measure of joy comes to the devoted mother when in her declining years she can see her children strong in mind and body, fortified in moral strength through a knowledge of God's commandments, and with the strength to live by his teachings with prayerful understanding. To see them take their place with honor in church and community life and rear families of their own gives her the joy of fruition. Her anxieties will not decrease, for she will feel responsibility for each new grandchild, but who wants the dull life where there is no anxiety? Her compensation comes as each of those she loves makes the climb to life's fulfillment.

The aging mother who has given the full measure of care and devotion to her children should look forward unafraid to her declining years. Her greatest desire will be to maintain her independence to the end of her days, but she will look longingly for words of appreciation and love. She should not want to hold her children near if greater opportunities are to be found in other localities, but she will be just as anxious to know of the daily activities of her children as she was when they were little and needed her care. Frequent letters and visits will give the joy that makes life worth living. Her hunger for affection and thoughtful consideration from her children is just as real as was their need for her when they were little, and this she gave unstintingly.

And so the cycle of life repeats itself. The laws of life that God has given us, if we obey them, make this pathway one of gradual development and joy in accomplishment. The loving, obedient child becomes the wise and helpful parent who merits, in turn, the love of thoughtful children grown strong.

The once-a-year observance of Mother's Day should only serve to stimulate in us a greater appreciation for the responsibility of family life. The possibility that this special day may become commercialized is ever present. There are those careless children who feel that they can make up for a year of neglect of their mother by lavishing upon her expensive gifts and attentions on this day. Mothers are appreciative and grateful, but nothing can take the place of consistent love and devotion. Flowers will fade, but the gift of a pure life dedicated to righteousness lasts through eternity. Modest mothers accept the public acclaim and special attention with a feeling of reservation and humility. Motherhood brings to them the greatest joy that can be known to woman. With that joy comes tremendous responsibility, and if she can feel that she has faithfully discharged her trust, she knows the peace and joy that passes understanding.

"Let every day be mother's day," where there is love and understanding between mothers and children and where there is joy in companionship and service of each for the other.

EXCERPTS FROM
CAMILLA'S WRITINGS

11

A Child of God

Keep the Commandments

We have a divine heritage. The song "I Am a Child of God" is one of my favorites. It sets the thinking of our children at a very young age to realize where we came from, why we are here, and what our future may be.

Salvation is individual responsibility. Our parents may have had wonderful testimonies and may have lived well, but it is our individual responsibility to make our own way to eternal life.

Gospel message is constant. The gospel message today is the same as it has always been: love God, follow Christ, serve one another, develop self-mastery and spiritual power, keep the commandments with the assurance that thereby God will be pleased and you will obtain eternal joy, never give up in well doing, continue faithful to the end.

Note: A small "bullet" at the beginning of a paragraph indicates a different source from the previous paragraph.

Salvation comes by the grace of Christ. See page 25, paragraphs 1, 2.

Taking on the name of Christ is a great responsibility. We assume a tremendous responsibility when we take upon ourselves the name of our Savior. As members of his church we are his representatives here on the earth, and we have the responsibility to represent him faithfully. We are all missionaries, wherever we go, whomever we meet. We are committed to seek after everything "virtuous, lovely, or of good report," and we can bring to the Church either respect or scorn. Anything we can do for Christ's cause in bringing the people of the earth to recognize him as their Savior is insignificant compared with what he has done for us, but it is our challenge. We must serve well.

The message of Christmas is love. We miss the spirit of Christmas if we consider the story of Christ as an indistinct, far-off event unrelated to our present problems. We miss the message of Christ's birth if we do not accept it as a living link that joins us all together in spirit as children of the ever-living and true God. In love alone—the love of God and the love of man—will be found the solution of all the ills that affect the world today.

Knowing our divine heritage imposes responsibility. Our pressing responsibility is to build up a personality worthy of our heritage as a children of God. We are of royal birth. Realizing this, we should strive to develop to our highest potential.

God's commandments are for our happiness. A vital thing for us to understand is that all the commandments of God are for our best good. They are not made arbitrarily to be a deterrent to joy and happiness, but are designed to help us avoid mistakes that will bring sadness and misery. Too often young people chafe under the restraint and in rebellion insist on "doing their own thing," when their lack of experience and judgment lets them make foolish and destructive choices.

Daily concerns obscure an eternal view. On the one hand, it helps me to be more diligent if I can see my place in the larger scheme of things and if I can be reminded what glorious things await us. But on the other hand, there is often so great a gap between our hope of heaven and the daily round of mundane activities that I must struggle to keep them in eternal perspective.

Each has a part to play. We do not know in advance just what part we may be called on to play. Esther was queen of Persia. Her husband, the king, did not know that she was a Jew. And when a decree had gone out that all the Jews should be killed, her uncle, Mordecai, appealed to her to step forward and plead with the king for her people. She pointed out to Mordecai that to do so would endanger her own life. He replied, "Who knoweth whether thou art come to the kingdom for such a time as this?" (Esther 4:14.) The question for us is what part we have to play in the great Cause. Every bit player is important to the outcome. Let us be ready for our stage entrance. Together we can do what no one of us can do alone.

Unchanging moral laws are for our good. To have lived from the horse and buggy age to the time of the jet airplane causes me to stand in amazement. When I was a girl, we made a trip as a family once a month to visit our grandparents in a town eighteen miles away. One day with a new span of fine horses we made the trip in three hours, and we boasted about it for months. Recently I crossed the Atlantic in that time. Even travel to the moon is no longer an impossible journey. The wonderful things that men are accomplishing can only be done by discovering the laws of nature. God knows and understands these unchanging laws. It is through them that he made and controls the universe. God's moral laws are also laws of nature and just as binding as any others. If we are mature enough to accept them as coming from an all-wise and loving Heavenly Father who has only our well being, our growth, and our development at heart, we will follow his guidance gratefully.

Prayer brings us nearer God. Our Father loves us, and he is as near to us as we will let him be. We should constantly seek his inspiration through prayer. If we ever have a feeling that he is far away, it is because we have moved away from him. Our first good morning should be to him, asking for his help in accomplishing the work at hand, in resisting temptation, and in giving love and service. If at the close of the day we can kneel and sincerely thank him for a good day, we can feel assured we are on the right track to eternal life with him. There will be a spirit of peace and well being in our heart.

It is safest to pay tithing regularly. See page 64, paragraph 2.

Take a generous approach to tithing. See page 64, paragraph 3.

Give children experience with tithing. See page 66, paragraph 1.

Small tithe is as acceptable as large tithe. See page 67, lines 1-9.

Live each day well. Every day well lived makes every yesterday a happy memory and every tomorrow a day of hope.

Endure to the end. I am grateful for the stimulation the Church gives us to realize that we can never be assured that the race is well run until we have completed our lives. It encourages us to study and grow and live every day worthily, that we may arrive at the end of our lives having successfully run the course.

• When my brother Henry was planning to go away to college in a non-Mormon community, my father said, "Son, I have no anxiety for you, if you realize that all truth is a part of the gospel. Analyze what you hear or read with that in mind. You will find that many of man's theories will be proven false. If you will keep yourself moral, stay active in the Church, and choose good companions, your faith and testimony will grow and I will have no anxiety about your taking the wrong path."

Gain Faith in Gospel and Church

Love God in every way. "Love the Lord thy God with all thy heart, and with all thy soul, and with all thy strength, and with all thy mind." (Luke 10:27.) In her heart and soul, a faithful woman acknowledges God's role in all things. Then, with her mind she seeks to understand the divine plan for this world. And finally, with the strength of her hands she undertakes to carry out the fundamental tasks of mankind, which are, to keep God's commandments and to give unselfish service to his children.

Nature testifies of God. I am not able to get around as much as I once did, and as a result I have looked at more television than I ever did in my younger years. In watching television I like best of all the programs that tell me about nature. Television is my substitute for travel. Through the marvel of the magic box I can be transported in an instant anywhere. I can travel through a telescope to outer space or through a microscope to the recesses of the human brain.

Whether it is bees or polar bears, whales or forests, I am fascinated by the fantastic variety and intricate interdependency of the various forms of life. I marvel at God's creation in its infinite complexity. I am much too unlettered to begin to understand the grand design of God, but like one who stands before a great tapestry, I can drink in its beauty and stand admiring its intricacy without knowing exactly how the artist achieved the effect. I know God's hand is in nature. I do not know just how God created the world, but I am persuaded that he did it, and I stand in awe and wonder at the majesty of his creation. My heart is full of gratitude toward a loving Father.

When we have obtained faith in the Great Creator, we are inclined to want to know what it is that would please God.

Christ will help us return to him. We are baptized members of the Church of Jesus Christ. We have been given the gift of the Holy Ghost to guide us on the perilous journey ahead. Christ has set the example and has left us a set of directions which, if we follow, will lead us safely back to his presence. He has not promised us that the road will be easy. In fact, he has told us that it will be difficult at times; but the problems will help us to grow in strength. He has assured us that he stands ready to help us and to guide us all the way if we but seek him in earnest prayer continually.

Salvation is a process, not an event. See page 5, paragraph 2.

Belonging to true church is no cause for pride. See page 5, paragraph 1.

All must seek spiritual growth. The Lord expects men and women alike to grow in spirituality—that is, to worship him; to gain understanding of the kind of being he is and wants us to become; to develop deep, abiding faith; and to live by divine principles of conduct. Of all we learn in life, the single most important knowledge we can attain is a firm testimony of the Lord Jesus Christ as our Savior and an understanding of the path he would have us follow.

Gospel is essential knowledge. With all the other knowledge that enriches our lives, let us not forget to include the knowledge of the gospel of Jesus Christ. When we think how fervently earthly parents want their children to grow up in faithfulness, we can appreciate in some small measure the great desire our Heavenly Father has that his beloved children may find their way back to him. Living the gospel is not the easiest way of life, but it is the most rewarding way.

Develop Personal Testimony

The true Christian has own testimony. The first essential credential of a true Christian is a personal testimony of the divinity of Christ. Our eternal life depends on our individual testimony. We cannot be saved on borrowed light. The faith of others may inspire us, but we must build our own testimony through prayerful study, by faith, and by obedience to the laws of God. No matter how strong the testimony of our parents or anyone else, we have the great responsibility of knowing for ourselves that Christ is our Savior and has given us the free gift of resurrection from the dead, but the degree of glory we merit is all up to us individually.

Some doubts are normal. Coming to grips with what we are and with what we can become is a part of growing up. Growing up is not easy; we are always plagued with doubts. I had the same doubts you have, likely worse. Most people do. That is not serious in itself, but if doubts stay with us for a lifetime, then it is a serious matter. We overcome doubts by daily self improvement. Your greatest asset will be a positive conviction and testimony of the gospel of Jesus Christ. If you have a firm commitment to follow this star with unwavering trust, numerous decisions will be ready made for you.

Put unanswered questions on the shelf. I used to tell my children, when they would ask questions to which I could give no answer, "There are some things you just have to put on the shelf for a while. Later you take them down and reexamine them. Sometimes then the question can be answered by new information or understanding that has come your way. Sometimes the question no longer holds any interest. Sometimes it must be put back on the shelf for another day. In the meantime, you just bide your time and go ahead on the basis of what you do know."

Truth survives man's theories. I remember while in high school we had a teacher of biology who introduced us to the theory of evolution. He traced convincingly the gradual development of life from the amoeba up through animals, monkeys to man, without the apparent need for God. He made it sound so convincing that I went home all excited to tell my mother and father of this great discovery. My kind father said gently, "Well, daughter, you will find as you grow older that the theories of men will never upset the truths of God." He had undeviating faith that all truth is a part of the gospel. Men once thought the world flat. How many theories through the ages have had to be revised.

Mormons are Christian. How often have you heard the question, "Are Mormons Christians?" We should be especially prepared to defend the Church on these grounds. One wonders why there should be the question. The nickname "Mormons" is no doubt the reason, and the fact that we claim added scriptures and continuing revelation is not acceptable to them. The fact also that we do not display the cross on our churches makes some question. Surely Christ is the head of this church. The name of the church is the Church of Jesus Christ. Every prayer is in his name. His life's example and his gospel are the foundation of our faith. His teachings are our constant guide.

Testimony needs nourishment. A testimony can be starved until it dies. The unhappiness of those who lose this witness strengthens my resolve to be steadfast.

Ordinances serve to reaffirm commitments. See page 21.

Faith is individual. Faith must be won with the help and power of God, each within himself. Even with help each must discover within himself those deep wellsprings of faith upon which life's eternal goals and achievements depend. Parents and grandparents may have perfect faith, but they cannot transmit it to their descendants.

People can be called of God though imperfect. I always tried to teach our children that people are not perfect, but that the gospel plan is perfect. I told them never to be let down by what an individual does. If a bishop or a General Authority makes a mistake, that has no effect on the truthfulness of the gospel.

Good books aid testimony. Some years ago I took a class on philosophy of religion at the University of Utah. Unknown to me, the teacher was an apostate from the Church. I went home from class each day confused and frustrated and angered by his criticisms of the Church. He made me so mad! I did not have the courage to speak up in class to oppose him, but there was a returned missionary who did, and I was grateful. Spencer would ask me, when I expressed my annoyance, "Why don't you quit the class, then?" I said, "I'm not going to let him drive me out of the class!" The teacher's challenges caused me to study more than I might otherwise have done. Elder John A. Widtsoe's *Evidences and Reconciliations* helped me work out the problems to my satisfaction. Perhaps the anti-Church teaching hurt the faith of some young people who were poorly grounded, but it caused others of us to struggle for greater understanding.

Scriptures deserve deep study. It is one thing to read and another to read, ponder, study, absorb, understand, and follow. In re-reading, I am amazed how much more there is to be understood with careful study. As we grow older we read with greater understanding and appreciation because of our life's experiences and maturing understanding. Recently the Gospel Doctrine class lesson was on the letter of the Apostle Paul to Philemon. Our teacher asked a member of the class to read the short letter through and then asked, "Is anyone ready to discuss it?" There was no response. Personally I could not really see much for discussion. Then the teacher began to tell about the personality of Philemon, a wealthy member of the church, and about his slave in whose behalf Paul was writing. He pointed out the methods of persuasion Paul was using to implore Philemon to take his slave back to service. He pointed out the lesson to value all church members, regardless of color of skin or station in life. The discussion opened my eyes. Every day I realize how limited my knowledge and understanding are and how much more carefully I must read the scriptures if I am to really understand and put them to use in my life.

Read positive materials. It is important for us to continually read positive, faith-promoting books to increase our faith. It is easier than we may think to develop a negative attitude. I know a young man who now is reading all the anti-Mormon books he can find and at the same time staying away from church and not reading the scriptures, and he has ceased to pray. What will be the inevitable result if he keeps on this course? I have heard many people insist that one should read both sides of the question, to be informed about the negative as well as the positive, but too often they then concentrate only on the negative.

Incentives help some to read scriptures. I had the privilege of teaching the Spiritual Living lessons in my ward for fifteen years, until I was eighty, during which time we studied the scriptures. We had a project for the sisters to read each of the books as we studied. I remember with gratitude that seventy-two of the sisters read the Book of Mormon; twelve of them read it through three times. In my experience every rereading of the scriptures brings new insight because of the added experience and greater maturity we bring to it. In three of the years the challenge was to read *Jesus the Christ* and *The Articles of Faith*, and to write a personal history. In June each year I invited all those who had completed the assignment to come to my home for a luncheon. Women expressed gratitude for the extra encouragement the luncheon gave them to do what they had always intended to do, but had not managed to do without that little prod.

Korean gold plates illustrate the plausibility of Joseph's history. In August 1976 we visited the National Museum in Seoul, Korea, to see the treasures that had been discovered in 1965 in the ruins of an ancient Buddhist temple. Nineteen gold plates, each about 14 by 15 inches, contain Buddhist scriptures engraven in Chinese characters. The plates are hinged together so that they can be folded up, one plate on top of another. Folded and secured by two golden bands, they had been placed in a bronze box along with other Buddhist relics in the eighth century. Chills ran up and down my spine, because the exhibit reminded me so much of the gold plates of the Book of Mormon. These Buddhist scriptures had been hidden away as long as those which Joseph Smith uncovered, yet they are perfectly preserved and easily legible. I had seen single gold plates with writing before, but never a book of plates.

Prayers of the people support their leaders. The evening in
December when Brother Haycock phoned from the hospital to
tell my husband that President Harold B. Lee was very ill, my
husband dashed out the door and into the car and was away in
an instant. I went to the bedroom onto my knees to pray. Half
an hour later the phone rang and my husband's voice in agony
said, "President Lee is dead. Pray for me." I couldn't control the
tears. It took me back thirty-one years earlier when the telephone
call came from Salt Lake to Arizona telling of his call to the
apostleship and the weeks of tears and anguish then. Being as
close to the Church presidency as we had been, I thought I
understood what the responsibility of the presidency would be,
but no one can begin to imagine the weight of the burden that
falls upon one man to whom millions of people look for guidance and inspiration. There is no room for any feeling of pride
or superiority. The burden keeps one on one's knees constantly.
If it were not for the faith and prayers and support of the wonderful people of the Church, it would be impossible to bear.

President Kimball accepted his call humbly. When Spencer
received the call to become one of the Twelve, he had doubts
whether he was a big enough person to do what was expected,
but I had no doubts. I knew he could do it and would do it. He
had been active in the Church all his life and had always been
a willing person. But as I thought about the terrific changes it
would make in our lives, I doubted that I was equal to the
challenge. I didn't think that a country girl such as I was could
measure up. I thought, too, of the sacrifices we would be called
on to make. We had labored hard to build up a business and a
new home in Arizona where we were known in the community
and respected. This would mean leaving our little puddle, where
we had been big frogs, for a big and frightening pond. Spencer
cried so! But knowing his talent and his complete dedication to
the Lord's work, I said, "You can do it!" I just hoped I could
hold up my end.

President Kimball was worthy of his responsibility. When I
recently reread my husband's life story, I had fun reliving some

of the great experiences we have had, and laughing at our foibles, but I also relived the sorrows. I asked myself how that man ever kept on through all he suffered, until I was reminded that what has motivated him all these years is a fierce loyalty to the Lord and to whatever calling the Lord has given him. He has done his best to bring about Zion. Perhaps he has come "for such a time as this." (Esther 4:14.)

I express my gratitude for the love and support I have received from my husband. In his ninety years he has served a long and honorable probation. Many people can say by faith that he is a great and good man. I say on the basis of the longest and closest personal experience that there is no finer person in the world. He is the soul of kindness and the embodiment of commitment to do right. He comes wonderfully close to perfection, in my opinion. It is the greatest sorrow of his life, and therefore the greatest sorrow of mine, that he cannot be out among the Saints testifying of Christ and teaching the right path. There is an aching frustration after a long and active life at being so limited in what he can do. He said the other day, with a spark of the old sense of humor, "Resurrection will feel so good after all this." With all his heart, with all his soul, with all his mind, with all his strength, he has loved and served the Lord.

President Kimball was a prophet. We are still small-town people at heart, and it is nearly overwhelming to be the object of so much attention. We know full well that the respect and regard in which Spencer is held is in large part due to his position, not his person, so it is humbling to be the symbolic recipient of honors only partly deserved.

I have appreciated living with a man who has an eager, receptive, seeking mind. He is always studying, writing, thinking, working. He has had unwavering devotion to the great cause of teaching the gospel of Jesus Christ and serving his fellowmen through his calling. I have appreciated his deep faithfulness and fervent testimony. Today, as always, the Church comes first in his life, and he has survived physical crises one after another after another because he has been determined to endure to the end, contributing to the full extent of his powers as long as he lives. That example is marvelous.

No one has known Spencer Kimball as well as I. Perhaps, therefore, my assessment can have some weight. I can say, without hesitation, that in this man there is great virtue. It is too much to say that he is perfect, but he comes wondrously close. There is in him devotion, and consistency, and power. I have sensed his struggles to know God's will, and I have sensed his peace in receiving the answer. My testimony of his prophetic calling has come to me in the same way it comes to you — by the whisperings of the Spirit. I know and testify that God called Spencer Kimball out of obscurity to perform a great work. He has labored hard to bring the world to a knowledge of Christ and the Father and to persuade men to do good. He has emphasized, as matters of special concern to the world, family, integrity, brotherhood among all men of whatever culture or race, the need for individual righteousness in withstanding the sensuality of the world, and giving unselfish service to others.

His knowledge of the truthfulness of the restored gospel and his integrity in keeping the commandments of God are basic in his life's activities. In all the sixty-four years of our lives together, I have never seen him short in any instance in living the laws of the gospel in completeness, always with love. There is no selfishness in his makeup. Consideration for himself comes last in every situation. I pray that we may take example from him.

God answers prayers. I served for a time as a guide on Temple Square. One morning as I was dressing to go, I was struck by a shattering question: "How do I know that Joseph Smith actually saw the Savior and the Father? How could I know such a thing?" I wondered how I had the temerity to say that this thing actually happened. I was terribly disturbed. I knelt and prayed about it, but left the house still troubled. I can still feel the sensation I had when I stood up to tell the Joseph Smith story that day, as I had told it so many times before. Suddenly I had a manifestation — a burning within my bosom — that was so assuring, so reassuring, that I had no question in myself that this was actually the testimony that is promised if we seek and really want to know. What is amazing to me is that I'd never thought of that question before. My testimony was just such a fact of my existence. And then the question and the answer came in the same day! I was not a youngster; I was a mature woman.

The gospel directs us heavenward. I wish to bear my testimony to the truthfulness of the gospel and to the joy and satisfaction one finds in following the path Christ marked out for us as he showed us the way. I know that he lives and that through his atoning sacrifice all people receive the free gift of resurrection. The gift of eternal life comes only through the ordinances of the gospel and keeping faithfully all of God's commandments. I know that the gospel was restored in these last days by a prophet and that each succeeding head of the Church has been inspired by Christ, who is the ultimate head of the Church. I pray that each of us may be wise and live successfully each day. May we know the great reward that is offered to us, that of eternal life in the kingdom of our Heavenly Father. My prayer for us all is that we may follow his admonition to seek divine perfection in our lives and endure, faithful and joyful, to the end of our lives so that we may worthily claim our reward in his kingdom.

 • I sincerely pray that the Lord will help us all to grow older gracefully, still vital and contributing and growing. I pray that he will help us develop that faith in him that serves as the drivespring to good works. I pray that he will help us improve our talents, to equip ourselves for work in his Cause. And I pray that we can fulfill our destiny as children of God, striving to be like him, loving and serving his other children, and building Zion.

Honor Parents

Family history is a kind of scripture. See page 35, lines 6 to 13.

Caroline Romney Eyring exemplified many fine traits. See page 71, paragraph 3, to page 72, paragraph 5.

Everyone should keep a journal. I hope each of you is keeping a journal. It is a valuable record of today. Tomorrow it will be the priceless history of your past.

Candor lends credibility. See page 39, paragraph 1.

Each generation is tested anew. The earliest generations in the Church were tested by persecution and hardship. I am of the third generation; many of us are now sixth generation or more. We have our own tests. Our forebears stand as models of strength and testimony, but we cannot stand on their testimony or their strength. We must stand on our own.

12

A Free Agent

Make Wise Choices

We are responsible for choices. Free agency is a law of heaven, and we must take the consequences of our free choice. Therein lies the importance of seeking divine guidance in the use of our free agency, that we may always choose the right.

Choice is unavoidable. See page 20, paragraph 1.

People in every condition have challenges. See page 27.

Choices are not unlimited. See page 20, paragraph 3.

There is no responsibility without understanding. See page 19, paragraphs 1-4.

Choices must be made with imperfect knowledge. See page 19, line 31, to page 20, line 5.

Choices can be wise or foolish. Our free agency, the right to choose, is a God-given privilege, but we must remember that the actual results of these choices may be far from what we had desired. If we choose wisely, with the long-range result carefully in mind, all may be well. But too often we choose foolishly, and the price we must ultimately pay is completely outside our expectations. What we do today vitally affects our tomorrows.

Results of choices may be delayed. See page 22, paragraph 2, and page 24, paragraph 7.

Choices shape life history. We write our life story as we go. If we create beautiful experiences for ourselves, rereading the pages of our book will reward us with happy memories.

Correct choices bring rewards. See page 23, paragraph 3, to page 24, paragraph 6.

Baptism is basic choice. Those who have accepted baptism in the Church of Jesus Christ have already made an important choice and solemn commitment to keep the commandments of God. In taking the sacrament of the Lord's Supper, they renew that covenant.

Make decisions only once. By deciding firmly that you will keep the commandments, as you promised in baptism, you need make decisions only once. You will have decided, for example, to be in regular attendance at church meetings, to keep the Word of Wisdom strictly, to be honest in your dealings and pay a full tithing, and to be morally clean. When temptations come, as they will, you will already have made the right choices.

Everyone struggles with imperfections. See page 27, paragraph 1.

Resist Temptations

Habits can enslave. Much is said by young people about freedom and "doing one's own thing," but there is no greater slave driver than a bad habit. If one realized the danger of the first cigarette, the first glass of liquor, the first drug use, he would be as fearful of that as of a rattlesnake. When you have seen the struggle of someone trying to break any bad habit, you know that there is no freedom there.

Make decisions just once. I believe I have saved myself a lot of turmoil by making some decisions early and once-for-all. That does not mean there will be no further problems, but it does narrow their scope. I recall that when I attended Utah State I went to a sorority banquet. Many of the girls drank coffee even though they were members of the Church. I knew I was not going to drink it, but I did not know quite what to do when the waitress came to fill my cup. Because I did not want to make a big fuss, I just let her fill my cup and then let it stand. I was too unsophisticated to realize that all I had to do was turn my cup over as a signal that I did not want coffee.

God expects chastity. Our concern is that youth may not be fully aware of the supreme importance of keeping their lives sexually clean. God has revealed through the prophets that chastity, among young people as well as older people, is as sacred as life itself. One of the most distressing lies being circulated among youth is that they can violate the law of chastity with impunity. No one can transgress this law and find peace without fully repenting.

We are bombarded with false standards. Young people are the hope of tomorrow. They are here on earth at a time when technology has never been so sophisticated, and the forces of evil are using that technology to bombard us all with false standards. False voices cry, "Marriage is not necessary. Anything that gives satisfaction is acceptable. Lie a little, steal a little, take advantage of your neighbor if it will bring you profit. Do your own thing."

Close your minds and hearts to the voices of evil. Take a long look at the future. Life is eternal. You are your own constant companion through every day of life and throughout all eternity. You cannot escape yourself. Some choices might give a thrill for the moment, but you must assess their lasting results.

Pornography can lead to unchastity. In most cases the body will reject harmful food with little damage, but if one puts improper thoughts in one's mind or looks at filthy pictures or reads vulgar literature, it is nearly impossible to erase the images from the mind. Pornography is the opening wedge to serious sin. Perhaps the greatest sin of our day is unchastity, and pornography propagates the pernicious lie that premarital sex is acceptable in society and before the Lord. Newspapers, magazines, television, and radio are all guilty of propaganda to spread the lie.

Thoughts produce actions. It isn't what we think we are; it is, What we think, we are. Our actions are the end result of our thoughts. "As a man thinketh in his heart, so is he."

Early dating is dangerous. Early steady dating limits opportunities to meet many prospective companions and poses a danger of undue intimacy. Petting in parked cars often follows, and more. The preventive for every evil is avoidance of temptation. Repentance is always possible and desirable, but better yet is the maintenance of personal purity.

Immodesty in dress will not attract good companions. There is a natural anxiety in every normal young woman approaching maturity to make herself attractive. Some are tempted to dress immodestly, but the man who is worthy to be her eternal companion is looking for sincerity, genuineness, and modesty.

Righteous marriage is a major goal. The object of each young person is to live clean and worthy to go to the House of the Lord with a partner who is equally worthy, to be sealed together for time and all eternity.

Righteous courtship prepares for good marriage. The choice of a mate is among the most important decisions of life. Choosing friends wisely is particularly important, and associations should be discreet. This is a time of great emotional strain. Fortify yourself and remember that God's law of chastity will be in force as long as time lasts, no matter what others may say.

13

A Well-Educated Person

The educated are custodians of a treasure. When we were young it was the exception to graduate from high school, and only a handful aspired to a college education. Today, with the sacrifice of both the student and many others, educational opportunities are available to nearly everyone.

The Church has demonstrated the value it places on education by the millions of dollars it spends supporting universities, colleges, and other schools. Students should take full advantage of these resources, remembering that the education provided in part by Church funds is a treasure over which they are custodians, with a responsibility to use it for good, unselfishly.

Education prepares for parenthood. It is sometimes urged that education for women is not as important as education for men, but there is no real difference. What we must be concerned with is preparation for life, and that preparation is education. Whether it is to earn a living or to rear a family, men and women both need to have the knowledge that enhances their natural talents.

Parents' aliveness to the world of ideas and art and science opens new vistas for children. Parents who plump themselves down in front of a television set without discrimination on what they watch reduce the likelihood that their children will achieve the things they hope for.

• If a woman buries herself inside four walls, she does not reach her potential. She needs to keep growing, and to keep aware of the world in which her children are growing.

Women should prepare for two vocations. Many of our young women will have little or no experience with marriage and motherhood in a model Latter-day Saint family relationship. We cannot assume that all of our women will marry, remain married, be physically able to have children, or remain in the home with them. Consequently, each woman should prepare for all of these contingencies.

Many will need to earn a living for themselves because they do not marry or do not marry until after some years of employment or because they have been widowed or through other circumstances have been compelled to assume the responsibility of the family breadwinner. A mother who must earn a living for the family in addition to performing the duties of motherhood probably has a greater need for education than any person in the world.

Education is more than vocational. It should prepare our minds, strengthen our bodies, heighten our cultural awareness, and increase our spirituality. Such education will improve a woman's ability to function as an informed and effective teacher of her sons and daughters and as a worthy and wise counselor and companion to her husband or as a person making her way in the world alone.

• Recently I had a letter from a young woman in Colorado. She said, "In view of the fact that the Church teaches that the greatest role in life for a woman is to be a wife and mother, do you think it is important for a woman to go to college?" You may know I told her of the importance of education. Every field of training will be useful preparation for being a successful wife and mother. No career needs more diversified skills. But a young women's education should prepare her not only for the responsibilities of motherhood, but also for the whole span of her life. She should aspire to the most effective use of her talents, first in the family but also in the wider world of service and accomplishment.

• See also page 60, paragraphs 2, 3.

Avid reading contributes to education. When I was twelve or thirteen, I was sent to live with my grandmother, who was alone. I loved and respected her. She was an immigrant from Switzerland and as hard a worker as you could find. She not only kept up her house at eighty, but also kept a fine vineyard, a vegetable garden, and a flock of chickens. She lived the gospel in its minutest detail, as she understood it.

She had been reared to believe that it was a sin to read novels, but I was an avid reader and loved stories most of all. In the upstairs room where I slept were some shelves of books that my cousins had left and that I felt compelled to read. I did not want to displease my grandmother, but I could not understand her attitude toward these stories. So I compromised by taking every opportunity to read when she was working in the garden or otherwise not observing me.

Broad reading educates. I used to read a lot, but I didn't read just anything. I relied on reviews of the books or on recommendations of friends whose judgment I trusted. I avoided things that were poorly written or morbid or salacious, and looked for books that were well written and would teach me about people. I used to read mostly novels, for entertainment, not for development. But reading did educate me. There is a lesson in every good story, if you look for it. If you read for meaning, you meet new ideas.

Education is worth sacrifice. My mother had the privilege of going only through the fifth grade, yet she became a good schoolteacher. I was midway through high school when our family became refugees from the civil war in Mexico and left all our property behind. From then on it was the responsibility for me and my brothers and sisters to make our own way through school. We learned that nothing worthwhile comes without effort.

Though we had no money, my uncle Carl Eyring, who was in Provo attending Brigham Young University along with his sister, wrote inviting me to come live with them and finish high school at BYU. That was most generous, because they were hard pressed for money enough to keep the two of them in school. The next two years at BYU were hard, poverty-ridden years, but a time of great personal growth. I prepared myself for employment as a teacher of home economics in the Church academies. One time I received a telegram from my father asking why I had not written home. The reason was that I did not have two cents for a stamp. But I could not give up school. Being a student and becoming a teacher were both my pleasure and my need.

Many of the people who came to BYU in those days were there at considerable sacrifice. Education was hard to come by and recognized as a precious commodity. That is still true. Many students today have chosen a hard road, but they are coming into possession of a fund of knowledge beyond the dreams of most people in the world. It carries with it great power for good or ill.

Education is not limited to formal schooling. As a young teacher, I planned to alternate working and going to school until I had completed a graduate degree in dietetics. As it turned out, I met Spencer Kimball and married instead. That kept me from finishing my specific educational goal, but it did not stop my being curious, nor did it stop my learning, because regular schooling is just one of the ways of becoming educated.

Reading books has opened a thousand doors for me. I worked through the Women's Club in Arizona to help establish a public library in the little farming town where we lived in order to open those same doors for others. We also benefitted from having a college nearby, which provided some community education classes. And I was always active in church teaching.

"To teach is to learn." I enjoyed the challenge to understanding, which is a prerequisite to effective teaching. I always did my best to encourage my brothers and sisters and my children to take advantage of educational opportunities. If there was a price to be paid, in money or effort, I considered it well worth the price.

I have found from my own experience, in taking courses at the Institute of Religion and at the University of Utah after we moved to Salt Lake City, that there is joy in learning, that it helps keep you young in spirit, and that, whatever it is— religion or Spanish or typing or literature—it enlarges our capacity for service.

• The Relief Society provides priceless schooling. Its course of study has offered religious training, homemaking skills, child development training, social skills, cultural refinement, opportunities for charitable service, and the choicest of friendships. Any woman who fails to take full advantage of what Relief Society has to offer is shortsighted.

Education requires curiosity. I have always hoped some day to be considered an educated woman. One cannot be educated in the full sense without a driving curiosity.

• I have always had an inquiring mind. I am not satisfied just to accept things; I like to follow through and study things out. Living in this world has proven to be a voyage of continual discovery.

Learning can give both pleasure and understanding. The process of education, aside from its pleasure, disciplines the mind and makes it our useful servant. I love to study; I love to learn. At one time I learned for the sheer pleasure of learning. Now in my old age I do it more for the purpose of understanding God's great creation and my role in it. As a result, I don't read much fiction anymore. In the past few months I have read a book of essays that gave me new insights into gospel principles. I finished the Book of Mormon again, which ends on a stirring challenge to be "perfect in Christ." *A Marvelous Work and a Wonder* by LeGrand Richards got me thinking about the urgent preparations we need to make against the troubles of the Last Days. And I have read several biographies, looking to see how God's plan works itself out in the lives of men. As I read the scriptures, I stand amazed at how I can fall so far short of living all the commandments and yet know that God loves me anyway.

Learning can be an avenue of faith. I believe that to love God with our mind means to pursue understanding of his world. Though we may have other gifts as well, all of us have the marvelous ability to acquire knowledge. We are taught through the Prophet Joseph Smith that we should "seek learning, even by study and also by faith." (D&C 88:118.)

   • Learning is a religious activity in the sense that it brings us to value the inherent goodness in people, to appreciate the world around us, to see the fruits of unselfish cooperation, to increase a sense of self-worth, and to feel a capacity to be of service to others.

All truths are worthy. Learning is not just for one set of people or for one time of life. It is a basic activity for all mankind. We are on earth to learn — first of all the principles of salvation, and then the secrets of the world, to subdue it and make it fruitful, and to delight the mind. The Lord fosters beauty, and there is beauty in all knowledge — not just in music and painting, but in biology and geology and mathematics, too.

   • It is our responsibility to gather truth of all sorts, not just truths of theology, but of everything. So long as we do not become vain in our learning, it is all to the good.

Avoid pride in learning. There is some risk in education, of course. It can in a sense become our master rather than our servant. If I may paraphrase a scripture: We have learned by experience that it is the nature and disposition of almost all persons, as soon as they get a little knowledge, as they suppose, to begin to lord it over others. Learning is one of the great sources of pride. Nephi cried out, "O the wise, and the learned, . . . that are puffed up in the pride of their hearts, . . . wo be unto them, saith the Lord God Almighty, for they shall be thrust down to hell!" (2 Nephi 28:15.) And he wrote also: "When they are learned they think they are wise, and they hearken not unto the counsel of God, for they set it aside, supposing they know of themselves, wherefore, their wisdom is foolishness. . . . But to be learned is good if they hearken unto the counsels of God." (2 Nephi 9:28-29.)

Nephi is not criticizing learning. On the contrary, he exalts learning as a good thing. He points out that learning has its risks. On the other hand, ignorance has its risks, too—just a different set.

14

An Equal Marriage Partner

Compatible ideas are vital to successful marriage. There comes a time when a young woman is pretty sure she has found that special one. That is the time for long talks together to discuss ideals and objectives. It helps tremendously if their ideas are compatible about thrift and industry, living the commandments one hundred percent, giving service, paying tithes, enjoying similar entertainments, looking forward to rearing a family together.

Romantic love is wonderful, but a bit of realism helps too. There are bound to be difficulties when two people from different homes set up housekeeping together. There needs to be a great reservoir of patience and much willingness to give and take. Unselfishness is a prime virtue in marriage. Each must be willing to go not 50 percent of the way in making adjustments, but 75 percent. Love must be worked for, developed, and earned continually.

• Compatibility is a very important thing; it is important that you have common interests, common ideals, and common goals. This is a foundation upon which you build love. Physical attraction, although important, is only one facet of love.

One's marriage choice shapes life. See page 26, paragraph 2.

Marriage can tolerate some differences. Loving one another does not mean always seeing things the same way. Sometimes a difference in style adds spice to friendship. I am a bit more restless than my husband. He has always been solid and unquestioning in his faith, and he has never been able to understand why I have to question and delve. The gospel is something he has few questions about, while I keep looking for explanations. His sureness has a kind of serenity about it; I wish it were as easy for me. But we seem to come out at the same place. We both know that the atonement is a living reality and neither knows how Christ was able to suffer for the sins of the world. I wonder how it actually happened; Spencer is happy to wait for the answer.

Wife and husband can share all blessings. Before the Fall, Eve was sealed to Adam in the new and everlasting covenant of marriage. She was a joint participant with Adam in all his ministry and will inherit with him all the blessings of his exaltation.

With the restoration of the gospel of Jesus Christ, we are blessed to know that as women we inherit the blessings and responsibilities of Eve, if we comply with the commandments upon which these blessings are predicated. Womanhood is an eternal and divine project.

Women can receive all blessings of the priesthood. See page 10, paragraph 2.

Emma's revelation applies to all. The revelation to Emma Smith in Doctrine and Covenants section 25 sets the pattern for other women too. She murmured because she felt excluded from some things. As the wife of the Prophet, she seems to have felt that she was entitled to be admitted into the councils of her husband and the brethren. But her responsibility was to support Joseph in his afflictions and to help him do the special work to which he was called.

Emma was assigned to teach, to write, and to learn. She was to focus on spiritual more than worldly things, to keep the covenants she had made, and to beware of pride. If she kept the commandments continually, she had the promise of a crown of righteousness.

The Lord ended the revelation by extending the admonition and the promise to us also: " . . . this is my voice unto all."

A wife should avoid problems with confidentiality. My husband and I were married in 1917, and in all those years I haven't sat beside him in a sacrament meeting a dozen times. His place has always been on the stand, and when our children were little, it wasn't easy to wrestle with them alone.

A woman must be severely self-disciplined when her husband is in leadership positions. She must realize that there are many areas he is not free to discuss with her. I have always been glad that when a friend in curiosity would ask me about selections of officers to be made or personalities or problems of any kind, I could honestly say, "I know nothing about it. I can tell you when I read it in the newspaper or hear it from the pulpit." I know that sometimes capable and worthy men have been passed by because they had wives who were not cooperative.

• I try not to know of any confidential matters, but there is rarely any problem because Spencer is so careful that often I am the last to know something. Out of an abundance of caution, Spencer does not even tell me things that are not confidential. It is probably easier for him not to try to remember which things are public information and which are not.

Be slow to take offense. There were a few times when my feelings got hurt. I believe that silence is the best reaction, not an outburst of anger. I would think things over and ask myself, "Did he intend to be neglectful, or is his mind preoccupied with other things?" There is no point in pouting or nursing grievances. It helps to develop a sense of humor.

Families are an eternal unit. So far as we know, the Church organization may not be found in heaven, but families will be. God joined Adam and Eve in the holy bonds of marriage even before they were mortal and commanded them to cleave to one another. Through all ages God has fostered the family, giving to men the sealing power so that families can be joined for eternity. The importance of our finding worthy companions and of temple marriage cannot be overestimated when we realize that our eternal destiny depends in part upon this sacred ordinance. Without it, we cannot have fulness of joy. With it, the future is boundless. There are some who, through no fault of their own, do not have that opportunity in this life, but no one worthy of these blessings will be denied them indefinitely. Life stretches beyond mortality, and those who live worthily will find fulfill-ment in the hereafter.

Woman has a divinely appointed role. A woman with her life sweetened by gospel experiences, enlightened by religious train-ing, and strengthened by the ordinances and directions of the holy priesthood of God is bound to have a different view of why she was born than do others. No matter how liberal or eman-cipated or sophisticated such a woman may think she is, deep down she knows she is a cherished child of God and the recipient with others of his children, both male and female, of all the blessings of a plan of eternal life. The day she comes to under-stand her role, to be comfortable in God's will for her, is the day of her giant stride.

To the man, it has been given to lead and to protect. To the woman, it has been given to love and to bear children. As man shares in the joy of children, so woman shares in the elevation that priesthood gives to life, for "neither is the man without the woman, neither the woman without the man in the Lord." (1 Corinthians 11:11.)

•Women are in no way inferior to men, but different in design and purpose. We have a God-given honored position and destiny to be the mothers of God's children.

• Women may not be without a certain restlessness in all of today's commotion about a woman's destined role. But if we understand the attitude of Christ and our Heavenly Father toward the all-important role we have as women, it makes us appreciate our God-given potential to be the mothers of God's spirit children.

• The special mission of the woman was clearly expressed to Adam and Eve when they were commanded to "multiply, and replenish the earth, and subdue it." (Genesis 1:28.) We cannot escape the responsibility of obeying this commandment, and not one of us would want to lose the joy and satisfaction that can be received in a happy family relationship. The knowledge that the gospel gives us of the eternal nature of the family is most precious.

Rejection of motherhood is wrong. In this day Satan is increasingly active in trying to lure women away from performing the most important privilege of bringing God's spirit children into the world, providing their mortal bodies. We hear much about emancipation, independence, sexual liberation, birth control, abortion, and other insidious propaganda belittling the sacred role of motherhood.

Women provide mortal bodies for God's children. See page 69, paragraph 1.

Motherhood has eternal consequences. See page 71, paragraph 2.

Family is the means to fulfillment. You need not choose between family and personal fulfillment. We should realize that in an active, surging world, the strength of one individual is of little consequence until it is linked up with others. There is no link so important and so eternal as the family sealed for eternity.

• Women are looking for greater challenges, but they would choose the lesser part if they were to give up a good marriage for another career. Women who feel it more exciting to have a business or professional career have not thought it through carefully. To be a mother and successfully rear a family multiplies your accomplishments. Suppose I had chosen to follow my chosen profession and had become a hospital dietitian. Think how narrow that would have been compared to the privilege of being the wife of a good man, the mother of four successful living children, grandmother and great-grandmother to many, and this is only the beginning. There is no comparison, only contrast.

Modern homemaking is freed from much drudgery. There are women who have a choice, yet seek another career than a good marriage. A small militant minority cry for some kind of liberation. Today with all the modern conveniences that have taken away most of the drudgery of the housewife, and with city living, which has removed us from farm chores, there is already one kind of liberation and more time.

Women unable to marry will be deprived of nothing in the end. There is great hope and consolation for women who do not have the opportunity of having children in this life. We are taught that our Heavenly Father understands our situation and that if we live and keep his commandments here, all things will be possible to us in the eternities. Life on earth is just a small chapter in our total existence. If we are deprived here because of circumstances over which we have no control, it will be made up to us in the life to come. If we realize that life lasts for eternity, we will have opportunity for fulfillments we did not have here.

• To the woman who marries later rather than sooner in this life, the promises and plan still hold. Her timetable before the Lord may be different. The lessons she has to learn, the tests she must meet for exaltation seemingly may delay the day of her "fulfillment," but each woman in the Church who lives her life according to the commandments will know eternal exaltation in its fullest meaning, which is marriage with increase. Living to claim this promise is every woman's business, whether she has taken vows yet or not.

• For women who have not yet found the happy role of wife, present satisfaction must of necessity come from a successful career and a fostering of the hope that in the future they may find the fulfillment God designed for women.

Marriage begins with a couple. When people ask what it feels like to be married to a prophet, I tell them, "I didn't marry a prophet. I married a young returned missionary."

Marriage is partnership. Marriage is an equal partnership between husband and wife. Each has a specific role. The father who holds the priesthood fills most successfully the role of director and protector of the group. Hopefully his position is never one of autocratic direction, but only of cooperative consideration carried out in perfect love and unselfishness. The role of a successful mother is a lifetime of dedication.

A successful home is our objective. I have covenanted to be a good wife and mother. If I have not made a success of that, I have been a failure in life. All of my other worldly activities are incidental to that one. But that is not unique to a woman. If my husband should fail as a husband and father, it would really not matter in the eternal scheme of things what else he has accomplished. He would still forfeit everything for that one critical failure to fulfill his covenants.

The wife is the key to her husband's success. A wife can be a real partner in her husband's success or she can be a millstone around his neck. To follow your husband's work, you may have to live in difficult places. A pioneering spirit helps. And if you feel sorry for yourself, try reading pioneer biographies and you will realize that your hardships are as nothing compared with what others endured.

Take an interest in your husband's problems and successes. Be quick to praise and encourage and very slow to criticize. If you can get to know the people with whom he is working and take a personal interest in them, you can become a part of his career and can often help him. How you see your husband and the importance of his work is reflected to others and helps determine their attitude toward him and the work he is doing.

You will be glad if you have always built up the image of their father to your children. Solicit their help in sustaining his efforts, which in turn are for the good of the family.

A wife needs to grow with her husband in understanding his job, but she also needs to find her own field of interest. She must find a zest for life by herself, in the things she finds satisfying and fulfilling. Wherever you are, there will be opportunities to study and learn, or there will always be interesting correspondence courses. Cooking, cleaning, washing, and ironing — tasks that must be repeated continually — can hardly be enough challenge. Find an interest and follow it to satisfaction.

• I offer a list of admonitions about being a good wife:

1. Be interested in your husband's activities.
2. Study to be informed.
3. Have a circle of married friends.
4. Take the attitude that you are on his side; be a helpmeet.
5. Support him in his church assignments.
6. Let him be head of the family.
7. Be a good listener.
8. Look for strengths, not weaknesses; criticism stifles love.
9. Communicate; plan together; have goals.
10. Find your recreations together.
11. Follow a budget; do not go into debt unnecessarily.
12. Learn to be flexible and agreeable in disappointments.
13. Have faith in your husband.
14. Develop a sense of humor.
15. Express love and appreciation.
16. Don't clam up if you are hurt; mend a hurt.
17. Pray together.
18. Make life an adventure.
20. Take problems one day at a time.

Children do not take precedence over husband. When children come, even they should not take precedence over the father. A woman's first responsibility is to be a true helpmeet to a husband.

A wife obeys her husband only in righteousness. I know a young woman who was incensed at being told she was expected to obey her husband, but she had not listened to the whole message. She was expected to obey her husband only in righteousness. That negates any concern for his taking unfair advantage, because her obligation is dependent on his acting righteously. The responsibility of the husband to love and cherish his wife, unselfishly, is equally binding on him.

Spouses need to go more than halfway. One develops character in service. Love must be worked for, developed, and earned continually. Unselfishness is a prime virtue in marriage. Each must be willing to go not 50 percent but 75 percent of the way in adjusting to differences.

I think both men and women exaggerate the degree of freedom that others have. Men often think of women at home as working to their own schedule, setting their own priorities, with resulting leisure time. Somehow the homemaker never seems to find that leisure time. In her turn she thinks of men out in the world of affairs making exciting decisions and meeting interesting people. Somehow the working man finds it all less exciting than she imagines. It is the age-old problem of difficulty in seeing things from another's point of view.

15

A Wise Parent

Home is a place for mutual respect and concern. See page 59, paragraphs 3, 4.

Spirituality in our homes. Our first responsibility is to develop our spirituality, to become the inspiration of our homes. The continuation of the family relationship in eternity is the ideal for which we are striving.

Our lives are bound up in our children's lives. I have come to realize that my family is the most precious thing in my life. Our lives are wrapped up in our children's lives. Their joys and sorrows, successes and disappointments help make up our life.

Love of family emulates God. I am grateful for the understanding we have of our responsibility to become Godlike in character,

118 The Writings of Camilla Eyring Kimball

to love our children and neighbors as God loves us. The family is important enough to call for our best efforts. The fullness of respect from good fellow human beings and from God comes to those who fit themselves to serve and then serve one another with love — and family first of all.

Homemaking demands great skill. No one should demean the role of homemaker. It is difficult to find another profession that takes more preparation and varied skills to perform successfully. The homemaker is teacher, psychologist, nurse, dietitian, cook, seamstress, maintenance specialist, financial manager, sociologist, and many other things. In fact, all useful knowledge will add to a woman's chances of being the perfect homemaker. Most of us are only partially prepared in most areas when we begin, so that we have to depend on on-the-job training.

• Thriftiness is an important skill. I buy food in season and clothing out of season, look for sales, and then plan the shopping so as to pick up bargains without unnecessary travel. Good clothes wear almost forever. I have worn one of my best suits regularly for fifteen years. Conservative clothes do not go out of style quickly. I have learned to make and remake and mend clothing. Unneeded lights burn up electricity. I cook a big batch of potatoes when I cook; then the second time they just need warming up, saving electricity. It is painful to see how much food is wasted in restaurants and at banquets. Sometimes I ask for a bag to take home part of my meal. If there is momentary embarrassment, at least it is in a good cause.

• People are sometimes surprised to learn that I do all my own housework. I do my washing, ironing, and cleaning. I tend my own garden. I freeze my vegetables and can the fruit. I love to do it. I do not mean to boast; I mean only that I am a very ordinary homemaker.

• When we were young we traveled and took the children along. We stayed in inexpensive motels and took our food with us. A lot of people felt they couldn't afford it. If they had known how we traveled, they would have known how we afforded it.

• See also page 5, paragraph 2.

Be careful in giving advice. When I first began teaching at nineteen, I taught cooking, sewing, theology, and English in a Church academy. In addition, I was asked to continue a community education course for married women about homemaking and child care. I was fresh from school with all the wonderful theories of the day, and so I was glib about telling them how to feed and train children. But after a long life as a wife and mother, I now give my advice much more tentatively.

Those who care for children shape their character. See page 8, paragraphs 2, 3.

Listen and communicate by good example. Are you a listener or a judge? We have all felt great relief from having shared with someone else our deep-set fears, worries, or joys without fear we were being judged. Many people seek professional help for these needs. Some fortunate ones can bare their souls to God. Some need help from every source available. Take time to listen sympathetically to your children, at any age. Keep the lines of communication open.

We parents communicate through language, but also through intonation or act, what we expect a child to be. When we show love, the child responds with love. When we are angry, he or she responds with anger or tantrums. When we take time with a child, that child is calm and wants to be helpful.

Children need supervision. I learned something from my mother's failures. When I was young and had to practice the pump organ, I learned that as long as there was some sort of noise coming from the organ, my mother, busy with her work elsewhere in the house, would not bother me. I managed to read novels all the while I was "practicing." When my children practiced, they often had their mother right there on the piano bench with them.

Offer affection and support. My experience with children tells me that it is important to be generous in display of affection and approval. There was a lot of hugging and kissing in our home. I believe our children have no doubts about our love for them and our loyalty to them.

We had high expectations—not unrealistic, just high. We found that our children tended to do just about what we expected of them. We offered support. When any of the children performed in school plays or athletics or on a church program, we tried to be there. We tried to do things with our family—travel, work, talk, play. And we allowed for growing independence. We never had a feeling that our children were of any less worth than we were; they are also our Father's children.

After we tried our best to influence them for good, we ultimately had to leave them responsible for their own choices. That means that we loved them even when they made mistakes. We cannot live our children's lives for them.

Parents desire their children's welfare. See page 26, paragraph 1.

Allow children to achieve independence gradually. A great challenge for parents is to judiciously loosen the bonds of parental authority, to make way for an adolescent's progressive need for independence and individuality. This poses the dilemma: how to give direction yet not interfere with growing independence.

• During the teenage years parents should expect their children to do what is right and try to extend trust. Parents sometimes induce their children into wrong behavior patterns by refusing to trust them. One of the greatest safeguards a child will have is the knowledge that his mother trusts him and that the family looks to him to maintain family standards and family honor.

• Protection too long continued makes for weakness, not strength, in the child. To be counselor and protector, knowing when to assist and when to recede into the background, that your child may learn to walk alone, calls for almost superhuman wisdom.

• When you see your children suffer, it is traumatic. You would spare them anything that is really difficult if you could, but that is the wrong thing to do. The important thing is to help your children be equal to their challenges. You try to instill in them confidence and independence. When my little son had polio and fell down, I had to hold myself back from picking him up. I had to let him pick himself up, and it was hard, mighty hard.

Overindulgence of children hurts them. A mother must learn to do intelligent mothering. This is more than highly emotionalized mothering, which showers love and affection upon children to the point of overindulgence. She must not be blind to the weaknesses of her children, for this might lead her to uphold them in wrongdoing. She must realize that a child's future, to a large extent, is measured in the mother's ability to influence and direct him or her wisely. In the home must be taught faith, self-control, honesty, and loyalty. The gospel of work must be a part of the child's training. The environment for the development of a child physically, morally, emotionally, and spiritually must be provided. We should constantly hold children up to their very best effort.

Teach children to work. Affluence and ease are perhaps our greatest challenge. Too many parents who grew up the hard way want to give their children the luxuries they never had. But hard work, sacrifice, and struggle do not hurt; that is how we gain strength and fortitude. Every child should be taught to work.

• Often it is easier to do a job than to accept the untrained help of children, but they can learn to do only by doing.

Teach children to contribute. Children have an equal responsibility to contribute to the preservation of the home as a refuge of security. There must be complete confidence and faith between parents and children, and the children's consideration of and obedience to the parents are essential to the peace of the home. If each has concern for the welfare of the others, almost all disagreements can be avoided.

• See also page 75, paragraph 2, and page 76, paragraph 2.

Mothers should look to their own needs. See page 77, paragraph 3.

The home should be the focus for both men and women. See page 9, paragraph 8.

Rearing children is preparation for heaven. In evaluating a situation, one must always take into account circumstances. One should not presume to assess the needs of another woman, but at the same time there are certain standards and principles by which all our activities must be evaluated.

The gospel teaches that marriage is an eternal principle ordained before the foundation of the world. It teaches that in our existence here, through husband and wife, the spirits whom God created will be given tabernacles of flesh. It is here that we prove ourselves and prepare ourselves and our children for the place we shall hold in our eternal home. We live for time and all eternity.

The mother who works has difficulty meeting other family needs. The growing trend of mothers entering the labor market is bound to affect the well being of the home and family. It is difficult to measure accurately the results of this drastic change in the atmosphere of the home. Each situation is different, but undoubtedly some of the problems of child waywardness and adolescent upheavals flow from weakened discipline and strained attitude in the home. When a mother and father come home from a hard day at the factory or office or schoolroom and are already tired, but are faced with the responsibilities of the house, it is difficult to give proper attention to the desperate emotional, spiritual, and disciplinary needs of their children. If the mother underemphasizes the home, it is inevitable that the husband, the children, and the community will follow her lead and all will suffer proportionately.

Surely no one could ever feel that the responsibilities of home and family are not a full-time, challenging career.

Mothers of small children should go out to work only for strong reasons. See page 71, paragraph 2.

Teach children that being a mother is more than having babies. Nature may endow a girl with the physical potentiality of motherhood, but to become an ideal mother will take the combined training of home, church, and school. Above all must come her own realization of the tremendous responsibility this sacred calling entails.

Let each generation play its role. To be daughter, mother, and grandmother is to make the destined cycle of womanhood and to know the joys, responsibilities, and development these experiences bring.

Love is the greatest gift. Nothing we can buy will last forever, but love will, and character. By giving love and helping our families develop the Christ-like trait of unselfishness, we can lay the foundation for eternities of joy with our family and with all those who inherit the celestial kingdom.

Mothers deserve continuing appreciation, not just on Mother's Day. See page 78, paragraph 2.

Family traditions are valuable. Traditions are not inherently good, but traditions that embody truth and righteous doing reinforce our good intentions. Traditions also provide a link to the past, tying us to those whose traditions we follow. It is valuable, therefore, for families to build good traditions. But what the traditions are may be less important than that we establish some pattern. Continuity contributes to a sense of security.

Family history can give encouragement. See page 36, paragraphs 1, 2.

Christmas is a time for quiet contemplation. See page 49, paragraphs 1, 2.

Family home evening unites families. See page 6, paragraph 3, to page 7, paragraph 3.

Relief Society serves women's and families' needs. See page 61, paragraph 4.

Church training prepares us to meet difficulties. I was born in a tiny village in Old Mexico. There were no hospital facilities. My mother was cared for by a midwife at home. I was born in a small, red brick home. There was no electricity. A kerosene lamp or a candle furnished our only artificial light. Transportation was by walking, horseback, or horse-drawn buggy. Maybe once a year we had a train ride in which a wood-burning engine pulled the antiquated cars slowly across the miles to El Paso, Texas, the most exciting experience of my childhood. There was no telephone or telegraph. A letter was an exciting communication. Radio, television, and movies were not in existence. Perhaps you are thinking it must have been a dull, unexciting life, but I think of it as a happy, interesting time. We lived in a close-knit Mormon community with close friends; grandparents; uncles, aunts, and cousins; parents; brothers and sisters. A community of happy homes. The Church provided our schools and our entertainment. We produced our own plays and had neighborhood games. There were community dances that provided vigorous exercise and fun. We knew everyone and were related to many.

Then came civil war in the country and finally so much danger that we were forced to leave our happy homes and all we possessed and flee to the United States for safety. I was just seventeen years old, and life suddenly became a tremendous challenge for survival.

The thing that made possible the transition from the safety and security of my childhood home to the new and difficult environment was the church training I had had.

16

A Sincere Friend

We are interdependent. The most fundamental need of every person, the thing that is indispensable to every human being, is love, the feeling of being of value to others. Our interdependence with others is the most encompassing fact of human reality. We need each other.

Choose good friends. My choice of friends has helped keep me straight. I have had friends who expected me to be good, and I have tried not to disappoint them.

We all need friends. Friendliness wins and holds as few other things can. When a person manifests the least kindness and love toward us, what a glow of warmth fills our soul. Whether we be young or old, rich or poor, obscure or prominent, we need someone who has an understanding heart. Lack of understanding erects barriers and impedes progress, while understanding generates love and furthers accomplishment. Relief Society should be an organization of understanding hearts, because we are sisters.

Give encouragement to others. We miss the mark in not giving enough encouragement to those around us. Not long ago I happened to overhear a conversation in which someone commented on my having given a good talk. Because I knew it was not meant for my ears, the remark gave me a deep feeling of gratification. I was amazed at how the glow of that simple compliment lasted all day. I think that a look in the eye and a firm handshake are worth a fortune in stimulating the spirit. I am trying honestly and generously (but without overdoing it) to offer praise and thanks. Sometimes I forget to do it, but I try not to forget.

Be friendly. Make friendships that will be stimulating and lasting. "If you would have a friend, you must be a friend." A happy, optimistic outlook on life will help to attract friends. A smiling countenance and a glad handclasp are a way of projecting your desire to make friends. Be constantly on the lookout for anyone who seems to be lonely and timid. That person needs your help. Determine to make the day a better one for someone else, and it will be a happier day for you.

• Old age feels as if you've come to a plateau and you look back at life and wish you had done some things differently. For one thing, I would like to have extended my friendships more broadly. My sister-in-law Winifred speaks to people in elevators and makes friends easily with strangers. Spencer had that skill too. He made friends easily everywhere. On the other hand, I have always been too reserved. But I sincerely want to be cordial.

Some who seem to reject friendship need it most. Friendliness and human kindness are universal needs of mankind. Without them, one is lonely or maybe embittered. With them, one's spirit is light and that person rises above the things that would defeat him or her. For one reason or another in every community, even in the Relief Society organization, there are those who feel rejected. Sometimes it is because they are critical and bitter, condemning other people or blaming circumstances. They may feel that they are unappreciated and misunderstood, that people are unfair to them. Or sometimes they remain on the outside because they feel inadequate, socially or otherwise. Sometimes something has occurred in their lives that makes them withdraw. Sometimes they are by nature diffident and retiring. Wistful people, they innately yearn to be a vital part of the group, to be friendly, and to win friends, but they remain lonely because they do not know how to freely mingle with others.

No matter what the cause, she who feels outside the group and who remains on the edge of things is to be sympathized with. An understanding effort should be made to bring her in and make her feel a part of the whole.

One of our common weaknesses is our failure to fellowship one another. Some time ago a man and his wife from Idaho came into our Sunday school class. When the request was given for any strangers to stand, the husband stood and after introducing himself said, "I'm glad of this opportunity, for up to this time not a soul has spoken to us. That would not happen if any of you should come to our ward." Needless to say, at the close of the class the couple were swamped with handshakes and greetings. We had needed that criticism.

Years ago, when we moved into a new ward, we met many people. I appreciated the acceptance and determined that I would be sure to greet anyone else who seemed new. So, seeing a lonely-looking woman, I extended my hand, introduced myself, and said, "I think I haven't met you." Her rejoinder was, "Well, I've been in the ward a lot longer than you have." Fellowshipping is a two-way street.

Church gatherings and especially the Relief Society should be the most friendly gatherings in the world because the Church is built upon the divine principle of love and brotherhood. The terms "brother" and "sister" so universally used in the Church are symbols of the family feeling that should characterize us upon all occasions. There is no organization more concerned with the well being and happiness of mankind.

• The world is full of lonely, troubled people who need a helping hand, who need a listening ear, a friendly visit, or a comforting letter. The watchword is "never stop growing and serving."

• Most of us have on our conscience a relative or neighbor or friend who really needs a visit or letter, some special message of love from us. I had an aunt in a rest home whom I visited too infrequently. Last week she died. I had gone to see her with a bouquet of flowers just a few days earlier. If I hadn't made that last visit, I would have been a long time forgiving myself.

Visiting teaching exemplifies Christian concern. See page 10, paragraph 1, to page 11, paragraph 1.

Prepare for visiting teaching. See page 55, paragraph 1.

Self-important people lack empathy. A thing that irks us about many so-called important people is that they are often so impressed with self that they seem blind to the needs and wishes of others. They are pompous and vain, impatient and demanding. They lack real compassion — the ability to share in the plans, hopes, dreams, and sufferings of others. One of the characteristics that made Lincoln great was his sincere compassion for the downtrodden, plus his personal modesty and profound humility.

Sincerity in friendship builds personality. The chances are that the thing that strikes you most about people who easily win your love and respect is the sincere warmth and affection they show. It may be the light in their eyes or their smile. It will often include the pleasant, friendly sound of their voice. People who possess a great deal of personal charm really like other people and are genuinely interested in them.

Learning to love and enjoy others — to give of yourself in personal relations — is the foremost key to building a radiant personality. Jesus Christ, the greatest personality of all times, said, "It is more blessed to give than to receive." If you can give warmth, love, kindness, and encouragement, if you can sincerely share your plans, hopes, and dreams with others, you will forge bonds of friendship that will endure, and you will be the one most blessed in the end.

Ask God for the capacity to love. Smile more; put warmth and enthusiasm in your voice and handshake. Love is one of the rarest commodities in this fighting, squabbling, envious, fiercely competitive world of ours. But it must be sincere. Don't try to "put on" love. Cheerfully express the love you do feel and go to your Heavenly Father and ask him for more. Learn to think of love and warmth as something you give, not something you get.

Be generous. Never suppress a generous impulse to word or deed. "Blessed are those who can give without remembering and take without forgetting." We should make a resolution to do some kind act of loving service every day.

Give love to receive love. Love is a two-way street. We give generously to others and receive love in return. Whom we serve, we love. That is my experience.

Capacity to serve is the greatest talent. Only some of us have talents of music, art, teaching, or sewing, but we all have the ability to give compassionate service. That talent is more precious than any other.

Service is the key to happiness. We should fill our days with those things that are of lasting value. Inner peace and happiness will come from remembering the times we have served others.

Mothers without children should seek varied interests. See page 73, paragraph 1.

We have responsibility to the community. Generally speaking, we consecrate our time and talent and service to ourselves, our families, and our church. However, our families live in neighborhoods and communities, which in turn make up the states and nation. If we take the trouble to see how a community affects the lives of its members, we will be more willing to work to improve the environment in which our families live.

• Women need to participate in community affairs, to be alert citizens and constructive critics. They should work in community organizations, do volunteer work, attend public hearings, vote in bond and school elections, and thus have the satisfaction of doing their bit to better the social environment. I am thrilled in visiting hospitals to see young women and older women giving service as volunteers. This is another opportunity to do community service.

Reach beyond your own family. The genuine mother takes time to reach out beyond her own children and sense her responsibility to help all children. Wherever a child is found cold, hungry, or in need of attention or care of any kind, a good mother will render loving and intelligent service.

Love for others leads to teaching them the gospel. Perhaps the greatest service we can offer others is to teach them the gospel. We have the feeling in our hearts that if they understood the gospel of Jesus Christ they could not resist membership in his church, because, as we know and understand it, the gospel is the way to love and happiness in this world for ourselves and for them.

Our contribution helps make a better world. I have a responsibility to strengthen others by my expression of love and confidence, thereby helping to bring about Zion. Zion will come about only through sacrifice and consecration of our best efforts. If we each bring our best gifts, cultivated and polished by faithful effort, together we can build a society where harmony prevails because we have put aside selfishness. I hope that over the years I may have grown a bit less selfish. At least I have tried. And I am reminded to keep on trying by the words of the prophets.

The gospel unites people of all lands. Each of us has gone through different experiences in life, sometimes because we live in different parts of the world; nevertheless, we share the most important experience of all, that of being members of the Church of Jesus Christ in the kingdom of God upon the earth. We are spiritual sons and daughters of the same Heavenly Father, and we share his love equally.

Abandon prejudice. I recently suddenly came to a clearer realization than ever before that we are in fact all brothers and sisters, and that the Lord holds out true brotherhood and sisterhood as a great objective. I realized that I still had some remnants of racial prejudices, and I wanted to understand the problems of minorities. I read Alex Haley's *Roots* to understand something of black slavery. Then I read George Washington Carver's *Up from Slavery*. I want to change.

Accept legitimate differences. Have we rid ourselves of prejudice? With all the diversity of our free society, we must be understanding and tolerant. There are problems to which there is more more than one answer; obligations may be filled in more than one way. While we should not be afraid to stand firm on principle, we need not disagree unpleasantly.

God values all people. We are all children of our Heavenly Father, who is equally concerned with each of his children. No matter the color of our skin, where we live, the language we speak, whether we are rich or poor, these things have no relationship to our intrinsic worth in his sight.

Cross-cultural sensitivity is essential. International brotherhood of Church members requires spiritual dedication, sacrifice, commitment, and integrity. It requires more than mere words. It requires that people resonate with one another's hopes, fears, and aspirations. It demands that one respect the high ideals and spiritual convictions of others. In communication of this kind, one feels the pain and happiness of another human being and comprehends another individual's quest for self-worth and dignity.

• When going across cultures, he who communicates well also understands the heart beat of a new land. Difficult? Yes, but important. The Third Convention in Mexico showed us the staggering consequences of failing to communicate empathically. Clearly this skill is an essential stone in the foundation of a Christian brotherhood.

All Church members must be prepared to give and take. This means a giving and taking that is psychological as well as material—a discarding of racial and ethnic prejudice, for example, and a development of empathy and cross-cultural sensitivity. If multiple Zions are to exist in doctrinal unity, while maintaining a certain cultural, political, and ethnic heterogeneity, we may yet have a great deal to learn.

• On our first visit to Korea in 1968, two Relief Society sisters had spent the day selecting a gift for me. In late afternoon, clothed in formal Korean dress, they brought the gift and presented me a lovely vase. I was so pleased that I reached over and kissed each on the cheek, as I had been accustomed to doing with the sisters in South America. As I did so, the sisters stiffened as if I had struck them. The mission president's wife later explained their surprise, saying that Koreans never touched each other in greeting, not even to shake hands. She thought, though, they would get over the shock. On subsequent visits we found that Koreans who had joined the Church learned to shake hands so vigorously that I wondered sometimes if the bones in my hand were crushed.

On our second visit, in 1973, to organize the first stake in Korea, the sisters presented me with formal native dress and asked that I wear it. The satin slippers were too small for my big feet, but otherwise I could. Two women came early to help me dress and fixed me just right. During the meeting they seemed upset and kept pointing to the bow. I kept trying to fix it one way and then another and finally seemed to satisfy them, but I never could figure out just what was wrong.

• In Ecuador, which is largely mountainous, five hundred Indians who live high in the mountains have been organized into a district with a number of branches. The president of the district is a native Indian. He and his wife were with us at the dinner given for officers of the mission in Bogota, Colombia. They were dressed in their typical Indian dress. His hair was in a braid down his back. His trousers were of white material, no stockings, just sandals on his bare feet. A typical knit wrap poncho served as a coat. The wife was also in typical costume. She wore a derby hat, which is universal in the highlands. Around her neck she wore a wide collar of many strands of gold beads. Her skirt was nearly to the ankle, with many petticoats of various colors. This couple had had fifteen children and only four had grown to maturity— eleven had died. The native Indian district president gave the closing prayer at the close of a conference meeting. In his district there was not a single automobile. Many of the people walk seven to fifteen miles to come to church over mountainous terrain. I heard President Kimball say that to see this Lamanite man take a position of leadership was the greatest joy of the trip.

• Sometimes our inexperience leads us to undervalue the efforts of others. Once when we were holding a mission conference in a Hopi village, I was invited to watch Helen Naha, a noted potter who had two children in the Indian Student Placement program, at work. We found Helen busy trying to get the fire and bed of coals just right for firing a number of pots she had shaped. She explained what her craft entailed. First she hitched up two bony horses to a small wagon and drove twenty miles to a clay mountain to get a load of special white clay. This trip took her three days. After mixing the clay with water to the right consistency, she shaped the bowls of different shapes and sizes on a hand-turned pottery wheel, then let the clay dry and polished it with agate stone handed down from her grandmother. She then built a bonfire of cedar chips and wood and fired the pottery a first time. The next day she painted free-hand designs using paint she had made over a long period by steeping desert plants she had carefully gathered. Some days later she fired the pottery again in a cedar fire to set the paint. I had sometimes felt that Indian crafts were rather expensive, but when I considered the time and effort and skill needed to make the objects, I realized that the price often represents only a pittance for long hours of labor. I learned something important.

17

A Growing Individual

Develop Yourself

We must learn to love ourselves. We are commanded, "Thou shalt love thy neighbour as thyself." Too often, I fear, we ignore the fact that the standard by which our love of neighbor is to be judged is our love of self. Who is the most important person in your life? Who is your constant and eternal companion? From birth to death and beyond you live with yourself, night and day, year in and year out. The most important person in your life is you. Our prime responsibility is to make of ourselves what our Heavenly Father has designed that we should be come. Take inventory in candid and searching self-analysis. It may be painful. Recognize your weaknesses. But on the other hand, don't underrate your strengths.

If you suffer self-doubt, know that most of us have felt that way. When I was seventeen, my family became refugees from the civil war in Mexico. I was the oldest of a large family, and we lost everything. From then on it was up to me to make my way alone financially, with a little help from relatives. When I went to Provo to school, the clothes my mother had painstakingly made me were all wrong. My skirts were up to my knees and in Provo they were wearing them long. My dresses were all cotton, and everyone wore wool. I suffered agony over my wardrobe. I felt so uncomfortable about my clothes that I made few friends. Whenever you submit to those stinging feelings of inadequacy or that feeling that you are not wanted, but merely tolerated, you are thinking about yourself instead of others. You are thinking about the wrong person.

Inadequacies are not fun, but they are conquerable. Difficult experiences will make you a better person if you learn and grow from the pain of them. It took me a long time to realize that my value was not to be measured by whether I wore stylish clothes. It was more important that I keep myself clean and look the best I could.

We have control over who we will become. Character is made up of small duties faithfully performed, of self-denials, of self-sacrifice, of kindly acts of love and duty. The saying that "as a man thinketh in his heart, so is he" states a fundamental fact. You can prevent wrong thoughts by keeping your mind on good things. You can also associate with positive-thinking people. Dream about and plan for the things you want in life.

• All worthwhile things have to be learned and then practiced. Habits are made by repetition. "What you are to be, you are now becoming."

• Wholeness of mind and spirit is not a quality conferred by nature or by God. It is like health and knowledge. Man has the capacity to attain it, but much depends on our own efforts. It needs a long, deliberate effort of the mind and the emotions and even the body. During our earthly life the body gradually slows down, but the mind has the capacity to grow even more lively and active. The chief limitations confronting us are not age or sex or race or money. They are laziness, shortsightedness, and lack of self-esteem. Those who avoid learning or abandon it find that life becomes dry, but when the mind is alert, life is luxuriant. No learner has ever run short of subjects to explore.

Don't waste opportunities to learn. Satisfaction in life comes from the ability to look back and feel success. If we make mistakes, lost opportunities will continue to bother us. For example, my mother wanted me to be musical, but I managed to read when I was supposed to be practicing. I now think it was stupid for me to neglect music, because I robbed myself of the ability to play the piano. I would not have had to give up reading; I could have had both. When I see my children and grandchildren who can play for their own children or for church meetings or for their own pleasure, I envy them.

I could kick myself for my failure to finish a college degree. I took courses nearly every year after we moved to Salt Lake City, but I took courses on impulse. They were all worthwhile, but if I had just planned a bit so they would fit together to satisfy a recognized major, such as home economics or literature, I could have had the additional satisfaction of a degree. When I had access to the university, I did not pursue a focused objective. Now it is not feasible for me. Maybe guilt does serve a function; it tends to stir me up to try harder tomorrow.

Use time carefully. We are all blessed with the same amount of time each day. Time is what life is made of, and how we use our time determines what sort of life we have.

• The present time is the raw material out of which we make whatever we will. Do not brood over the past or dream idly over the future, but seize the instant and get your lesson from the hour. Great men have always been misers of moments.

• See also page 26, paragraph 4.

Be open to other views. I think the Romneys have a trait of being bossy. My mother had it and nearly all of her children have it. Mother wanted us to do what she wanted us to do; there was no question about that. I recognize that I am a bit opinionated, too, but I truly want a broad perspective. I try to get others' points of view and to understand them, and I am willing to accept a better view when I find it. But change goes a bit against the grain.

Have an interest beyond work. Everyone should have an interest to occupy his leisure hours, something useful to which one turns with delight. It may be in the line of one's work or otherwise, but one's heart must be in it.

Each day one should have accomplished something special that need not be repeated tomorrow. Just to prepare three meals a day and keep the house clean does not completely satisfy. If one plans carefully, there should be some time for good reading or other mental development, some act of special service to neighbor or in church capacity. Careful planning is important; having a goal helps one on the road to accomplishment.

• Each of you has things you've Gotta Do, and things you Oughta Do, but life will be frustrating if you don't have time for something you Wanta Do, something creative, a hobby or recreation.

• I love to work in the yard. That is my therapy. I go out early in the morning, after Spencer goes to his office, and spend two or three hours puttering around, nurturing the flowers and vegetables. I like to get my hands in the dirt. I take pride in my yard. I have lots of roses; the Peace Rose is my favorite.

• Never stop growing mentally. Have a special interest that will continue to challenge you as long as you live. There are so many things to learn, so much to read and study. Never let household chores prevent you from being a challenging companion. Keep a lively interest in people and the world around you.

Painting leads to appreciation of nature. A few months ago I took up painting. When someone asked why, I had to say, "What else can you take up at ninety-two?" Something I had always wanted to do was to capture my beautiful backyard in a painting. And so after I had said that enough times, one of my friends arranged for a teacher and a weekly class and I started to paint. I thought painting would be easy until I tried it. But my art teacher is ideal. She helps without making me feel stupid. First

I painted my backyard and then a vase of flowers, and then I borrowed ideas from pictures in books. Painting has opened my eyes. I have a new appreciation not only for the painter's skills, but for nature itself, after having tried to capture in oils what I see.

I think that my paintings are about like my mother's. When she was young her father said, "Caddy, a person could kneel down and worship your painting without committing a sin, because it resembles nothing 'that is in heaven above, or in the earth beneath, or in the water under the earth.'"

Set goals. There are times when we are mired in everyday life and don't see the larger picture. It is in anticipation of those times that we must write our ultimate desires and our broad goals. Then we must break these larger goals down into smaller and smaller chunks until our dreams and our daily lives are in harmony.

Pursue specific goals. A person keeps from getting stale by having some objective, by reading and writing and talking in pursuit of a plan. We need to be always learning. I don't think of heaven as a place where there is nothing more to do. I think we'll still want objectives.

Keep growing. Some people feel that their responsibilities stifle them. I feel that fulfilling obligations is the most direct opportunity to grow—the very best way. Any woman should be alive to opportunities—alive to public interests, to her family, to growth from Church service. Life is so interesting, it worries me that I can't get it all done. And I have no patience with women whose lives bore them.

• Keep growing; there is no time to vegetate. Every success will give you more self-confidence. We are here to succeed.

• Most of us underrate ourselves. We are children of God, of royal heritage, but we seldom reach our full potential. We operate below capacity and may continue to do so until we realize we must be our own self-starter. We cannot blame anyone else for our failures.

Feelings of inadequacy have many causes. What are some of the causes of feeling inadequate?

• Not being appreciated as a child
• A history of failures
• Being compared adversely to someone else
• Illness or disability that convinced us we could not succeed
• A traumatic childhood experience that left us shaken and insecure
• Parents or friends who unfairly expected more from us than we could achieve.

For one reason or another we may carry into adulthood excess baggage of negative feelings about ourselves. We may be too timid to reach out boldly.

We receive confirmation of value when we act unselfishly. We all seek for confirmation of our value. But this confirmation rarely comes except to those whose actions merit support and encouragement. Love begets love. Thus the key to positive feelings about ourselves lies in our own hands. When we reach out and give of ourselves to others (though this may be a frightening thing to do), their response of gratitude and appreciation clearly communicates to us that we are worthwhile and useful. We are then more sure of ourselves and more willing to reach out in compassionate service. If we can chase away feelings of inadequacy for the moment and think about those around us, those feelings will diminish. It is the Lord's way.

Travel opens the mind. See page 12, paragraphs 4, 5.

Television can be educational. I'd still like to travel, to see the world, but I have to do it now by television. I have been able through that marvel to visit every part of the world and see things I could not have seen even by personal travel. Television has also given me a new awareness of the incredible complexity of nature and of the interdependency of God's creatures. I thrill to see the distant galaxies and realize that some are inhabited and that creation goes on and on. I guess I'm not satisfied with "what." I also want to know "why."

Everyone needs time alone. There is a quality of being alone that is incredibly precious. Every woman should have some time each day in solitude for quiet contemplation, an hour for renewal and appraisal of self, for prayer, music, a centering line of thought and study. Arranging a bowl of flowers in the morning can give a sense of quiet in a crowded day, like writing a poem or saying a prayer. What matters is that for a time one be inwardly attentive.

We need simplification in our lives. In an affluent and competitive society we should ask ourselves how little can we get along with, not how much can we get.

• The family is first priority for women, but each woman needs to have a little time for herself. Husbands need to understand that. If they make sacrifices to give their wives time, it ultimately redounds to their good too.

Find Joy Despite Problems

Problems are universal. Each of us has to deal with the conditions life gives us. To one person the challenge may be ill health; another may have a difficult marriage; a third may struggle for faith; still another may have a hot temper to overcome. Perhaps to some the challenge is that life is just too easy, that "all is well in Zion." I believe we will be judged by God according to his knowledge of our challenges. And we may well be surprised, if we get to heaven, to see what else is there. Our basis for judgment is so limited that we are likely to make a large share of mistakes. Our task is just to do the best we can. I know the Lord will be fair with us — more than fair; I know he will be generous, if we have given serious effort to do his will.

God knows our problems. I have great confidence in our Heavenly Father's justice and mercy. He knows us, he knows our intent, he knows our difficulties, and he will reward us for every righteous effort and forgive us wherein we are not responsible. He loves us and wishes us to be happy. He is always near, and his door is always open for us to discuss our problems. When we cry for help, we can feel his influence. He will inspire us to overcome our difficulties.

Suffering promotes empathy. It can be a blessing for us to sometimes receive a real shake-up and know what other people's sorrow is. When I think my family is having a bad time and a lot of sickness and financial problems, I always look around and say, "My goodness, we're not nearly as bad off as many other people who live close to us." We can always find someone whose cross is heavier than ours. Others are standing it and so can we.

Problems are challenges. Our Heavenly Father loves us and has given us opportunity to live in this world and develop our potential. He expects us to accept problems and master them. Each of us, man or woman, married or single, has difficulties.

• God has not promised us that the road will be easy. In fact, he has told us that it will be difficult at times, but that problems will help us to grow in strength. He has assured us that he stands ready to help us and to guide us all the way, if we but seek him in earnest prayer continually.

• Life has been full of problems and disappointments. I was a war bride of the First World War. We started our married life with no financial assets. We went through the Depression of the 1930s, losing all we had accumulated up to that time. Two sons and a son-in-law were in the Second World War. We have had our share of sickness, including a son with polio and many operations. But through it all, the joys and successes outweigh the problems. I would not choose to go over the road again, but I have only gratitude for the past experiences.

Struggle gives strength. See page 18, paragraph 7.

We need heroes. We need heroes, people whose life pattern we can emulate. If we examine others' lives, we learn how they have coped with problems and we can take courage in our own difficulties.

Mature adjustment to problems brings happiness. We should not take our luxuries for granted or consider them all-important. Happiness is achieved in individuals, not by flights to the moon or Mars, but in the satisfaction of mature adjustment to life as we find it.

• In pioneer days nearly every family had its share of typhoid fever patients. Contaminated water, myriads of flies, poor sanitation, few doctors and hospitals or preventative remedies caused frequent epidemics of communicable diseases. Double and even triple funerals were common in small country towns. My husband and my brother Henry both suffered typhoid fever and the treatment of a long starvation period. Both survived. Today this disease is a rarity on our country.

On the outskirts of our little town in Mexico was an old dilapidated building known as the pesthouse. Victims of smallpox were banished there, much as lepers in Palestine at the time of Christ. The disease was common. My husband suffered from it soon after our marriage; he has 125 pocks on his face and neck. Thanks to vaccination, no one ever need suffer smallpox again.

My mother's youngest brother lost the use of one leg through polio. My youngest son contracted that disease also. The Salk vaccine has made such suffering unnecessary.

Cancer has played havoc in our family, with many of our close relatives dying from that cause and my husband's voice being nearly lost.

A sense of humor helps us face problems. In the face of difficulty, look for the humorous side of things. Of course, always try to laugh with other people, not at them. Learn to laugh at yourself. Don't take yourself too seriously.

• The gospel way of life is a happy, peaceful way, a way of joy. A long face and doleful attitude are not prerequisite to a religious life.

Hymns calm the mind. If something worries me so that I cannot sleep, I just start singing the hymns in my mind. I find it the most successful way to dispel my worries.

Problems can be overcome. Forget self-pity and look for mountains to climb. Everyone has problems. The challenge is to cope with those problems and get our full measure of joy from life.

Happiness is achieved, not found. There are those who think there is something that will make them happy, if they can just get hold of it. They expect happiness to happen to them. They don't see that it is something they must attain.

• Some who have visited Palestine because it is where Jesus walked return saying, "I wish I hadn't gone. There is so much poverty and dirt." Emerson said, "Though we travel the world over to find the beautiful, we must carry it with us or we find it not."

• The happy life is not ushered in at any age to the sound of drums and trumpets. It grows upon us year by year, little by little, until at last we realize we have it. You do not find the happy life. You make it.

• I have often thought what a surprise it will be for the suicide to wake up and find he has carried all his problems right along with him. He must start exactly where he left off, with an added serious problem.

Happiness comes from living the gospel. True happiness is obtained only by following the basic model of life that has been outlined for us in the gospel plan of Christ. In this plan, Christ teaches that man is that he might have joy, and also that wickedness never was happiness. (See 2 Nephi 2:25; Alma 41:10.)

• Happiness is a treasure no one else can give you. You must give it to yourself. No one is born happy. It is an achievement brought about by inner productiveness. It comes not from ease or riches or the praise of men, but from doing something worthwhile. Happiness comes of the capacity to feel deeply, to enjoy simply, to think freely, and to be needed. It comes from conforming our lives to those things which set our minds at rest and our hearts at peace.

Exercise discretion in undertaking activities. I met a friend on the street. In a visit of not more than five minutes she told me she was employed outside the home; that she had four children, a husband, and an aged mother-in-law living in the home for whom she was responsible; that she was taking singing lessons and accepting invitations to sing in public; and that she was a class leader in Relief Society, active in PTA and partially active in a service organization. She also told me that the strains of her life were almost more than she could bear and that they were robbing her of much of the joy of living.

One must learn to discriminate. As to each activity, ask yourself whether it is really worth the time and energy that will be required. Are you spreading yourself too thin?

• In efforts to prove themselves the equal of men, some women have been drawn into competing with them in their outward activities, to the neglect of their own inner springs. What a circus act we women sometimes perform with our lives. It puts the trapeze artist to shame. The life of multiplicity leads not to unification, but to fragmentation.

Seek a realistic attitude. Some people are foolish optimists and some are pessimists. A combination that makes us realists is the safer position.

Look for the good. Look at your attitude. Is this a miserable day or a day of opportunity? Do you look for the good in your family and friends, or have you already marked them off?

There is exhilaration in meeting your own expectations. Do the things that make you feel good about yourself. Meet your own expectations. If you have something that needs to be done — a lesson to prepare, a household job that should be done, a sick friend you should visit — take yourself in hand and accomplish the task. Enjoy the experience of feeling in charge of yourself; it is exhilarating.

Be aware of your own achievements. When things go wrong, they call attention to themselves, but when things run well, we must actively bring them to consciousness. When you do something you are proud of, dwell on it a little. It is amazing the feeling of satisfaction that comes when we do what we know we should.

Spontaneity enlivens. I love the spontaneous dancing and singing of older women in the Pacific islands. It seems to keep them young and happy. We have become too inhibited and fearful of what people will think and say about us.

Endure to the End

Accept what each stage of life offers. Each phase of life is preparation for the next stage. Our responsibility is to recognize the opportunities that belong to each stage and not always be looking longingly forward or backward. We old people need to appreciate what life has already given us and realize that we can still give what Christ has directed us to give — service and love.

The elderly need mental stimulation. It's important for a woman to stay alive intellectually. It is so easy to get lazy when you're older and not really be stimulated to read widely and make the best use of time.

• It is important to grow intellectually and widen one's field of interest. A fact about getting older that saddens me is that learning is more difficult and there is still so much one wants to learn. Old people desperately need stimulation. If nothing stirs our attention, we can become uninterested in everything. Unless old people die suddenly, there comes a time when they stop reading and analyzing and speculating, and all they're interested in is food and warmth and freedom from pain. Maybe we can't completely stave off that deterioration, but we should struggle to stay mentally alive. And those who love old people should try to help them stay involved in the world. I have the great advantage of someone to live with me, family who visit me nearly every day, friends and neighbors who include me in their activities. We, old and young, have a tremendous responsibility to each other to give fellowship and encouragement.

• For us who are older, the challenge to succeed continues. Sometimes I feel frustrated at how little I know, when there is so much to learn and to do.

• See also page 61, paragraph 2.

The elderly can give as well as receive. I have an elderly friend who is facing old age with courage, intellectual ambition, and loving interest in others. She is an artist and always has several projects in process—a picture she is painting, ceramics she is designing, knitting, crocheting, or other needlework. Recently, when macrame knotting was introduced in Relief Society, she was eager to learn it. She is a real student of the gospel and always ready to contribute opinion and experiences to enrich the discussion. She regularly makes apple pies for friends. If a neighbor is ill, she is the first to bring not only concern but also a bowl of hot soup. Even for casual, unexpected guests, she has a cookie, a piece of candy, or a gift to offer. What a wonderful way to live one's later years.

• I know that older people serve as role models for younger people. I am not sure I am equal to that challenge, but it really isn't a matter of choice. Some people are much better models than others. For example, I can think of no more marvelous example of endurance and faithfulness than Spencer. Considering all the things he could have complained about, I think he was remarkably uncomplaining.

• I am flattered when people are willing to listen to an old lady, because it is said that old age is when you know all the answers, but nobody asks you the questions.

• When I was young I anticipated birthdays, seeing them as a mark of advancement and as opening the door to new opportunities. Then in middle age I dreaded birthdays, because they represented the closing of some doors and the approach of debilitating old age. But as I got older still—to the "My, but you're looking wonderful!" stage—I started to look forward to birthdays again, because each birthday marks something of an achievement, that I have managed to hang on through one more cycle of the seasons.

Except for a little pride in surviving, I can say from some experience that old age is not a status to envy, because there's not much future in it.

Values become simpler in old age. The older I grow, the more I live for family and church. Other things grow less important in comparison to my relationship with the Lord and with his children and mine.

• There is a measure of satisfaction that as we get older we keep coming closer and closer to "enduring to the end" by being faithful to the important values in life.

Old age is not funny. I can take a little teasing, but people need to remember that the problems of growing old are not really very funny to those who have them.

Dependency is the burden of the aged. It is no fun to grow old; I don't recommend it. The hardest thing in the world is to have people do things for me. Sometimes it seems like I'm drowning in debts to people for their kindnesses. But life is still enjoyable. I love my family. I love to travel and meet with the Saints and feel their enthusiasm and love. I have my home and garden and books and a bit of a sense of humor. I still have my eyes to the future.

• At least old age is a condition soon over. But I have absolute horror of being bedfast and having to be waited on hand and foot. If that ever happens, you're going to have to hear me grumble all the time. My greatest desire is that when I can't take care of myself at all, the Lord will quietly close the door.

I used to garden and put up peaches and cook meals, but I can't anymore. And that frustrates me. But other people fill my needs and I am most grateful for that, even though it is hard to be so dependent and to lose my privacy.

One of the hardest things is loss of memory. I sometimes go from one room to another and can't recall why I went there. And forgetting leads to anxiety about what it is that I am forgetting. I worry about whether there are important things I no longer recall, and whether I will eventually forget who I am and what I am supposed to do, and whether I will embarrass myself and those around me.

Endure to the end. When I was a young girl I noted that the testimonies of elderly people often closed with a prayer "that I may remain faithful to the end." I asked myself, "Is there no time when we can feel we have it made?" Now, at my age, I understand that there is no time we can relax. Sometimes the last years are the most trying and difficult. But if we constantly look about us for those who may be having an even more difficult time than we and help to cheer their way, then we are continuing the path that Christ marked out. The over-all message of the gospel is love and peace. At every age we need to do our part to bring about Zion.

Dying need not be fearsome. I don't dwell on dying, but I know that death is not far away, and so my plans are short-range ones. I have no fear of dying, but I am concerned that I may not have been valiant enough to be with my darling again, and there is nothing I want more than to be with him.

Index